Coloring Books For Toddlers

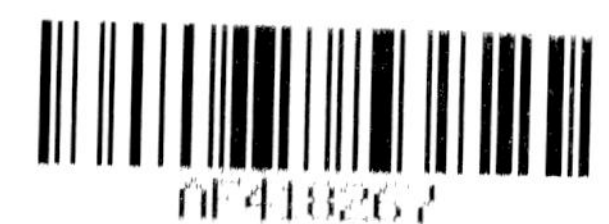

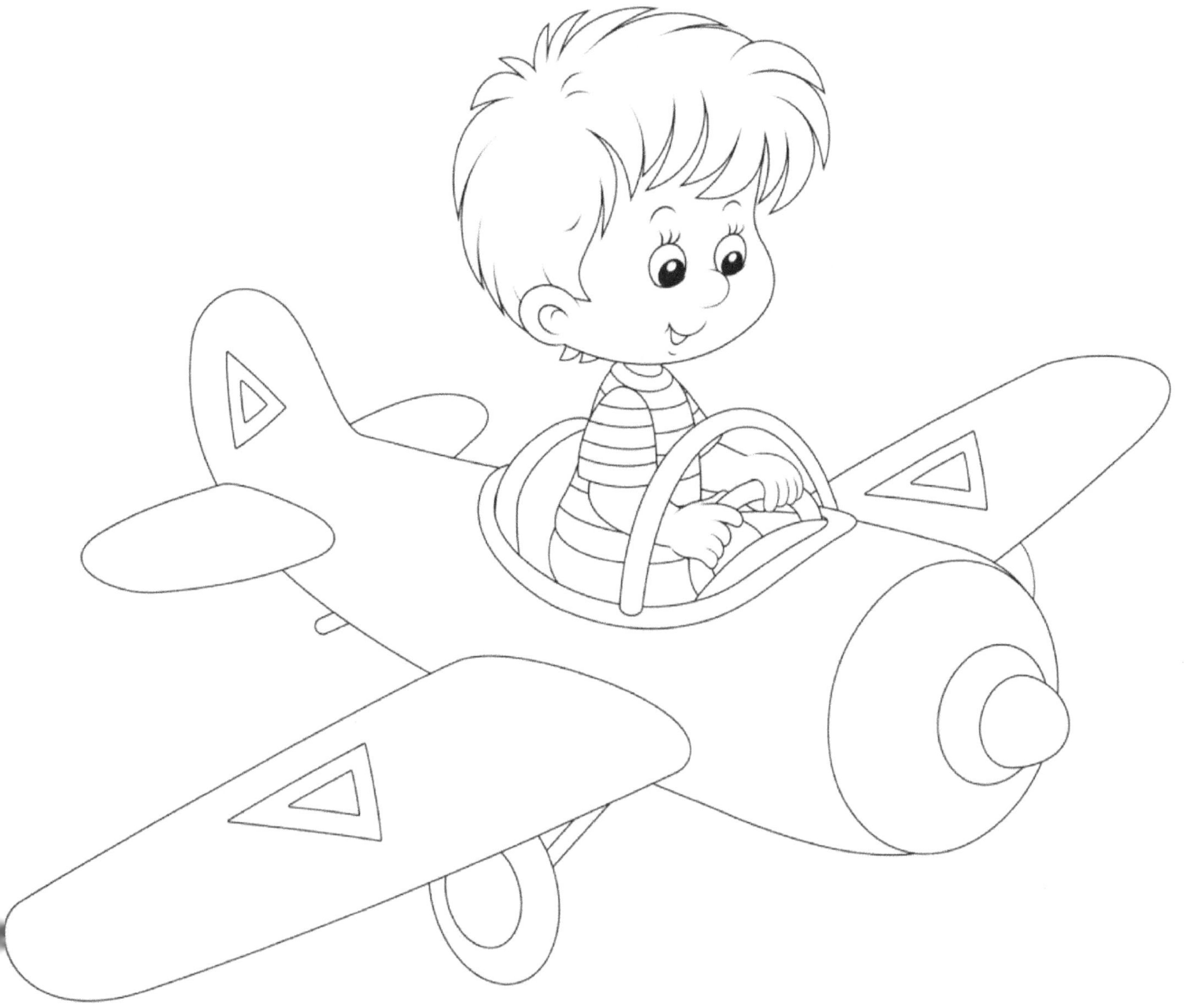

By
Happy School

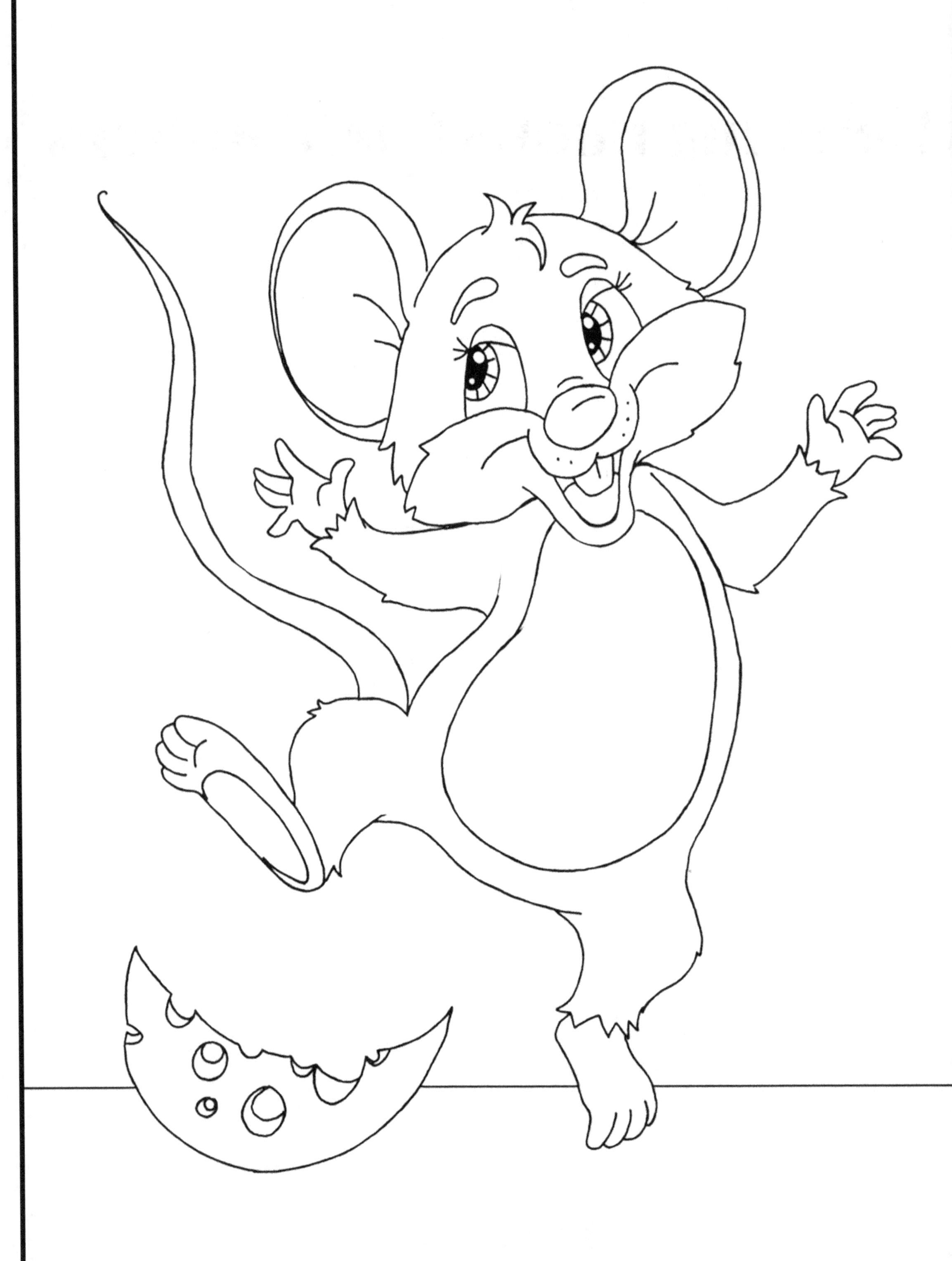

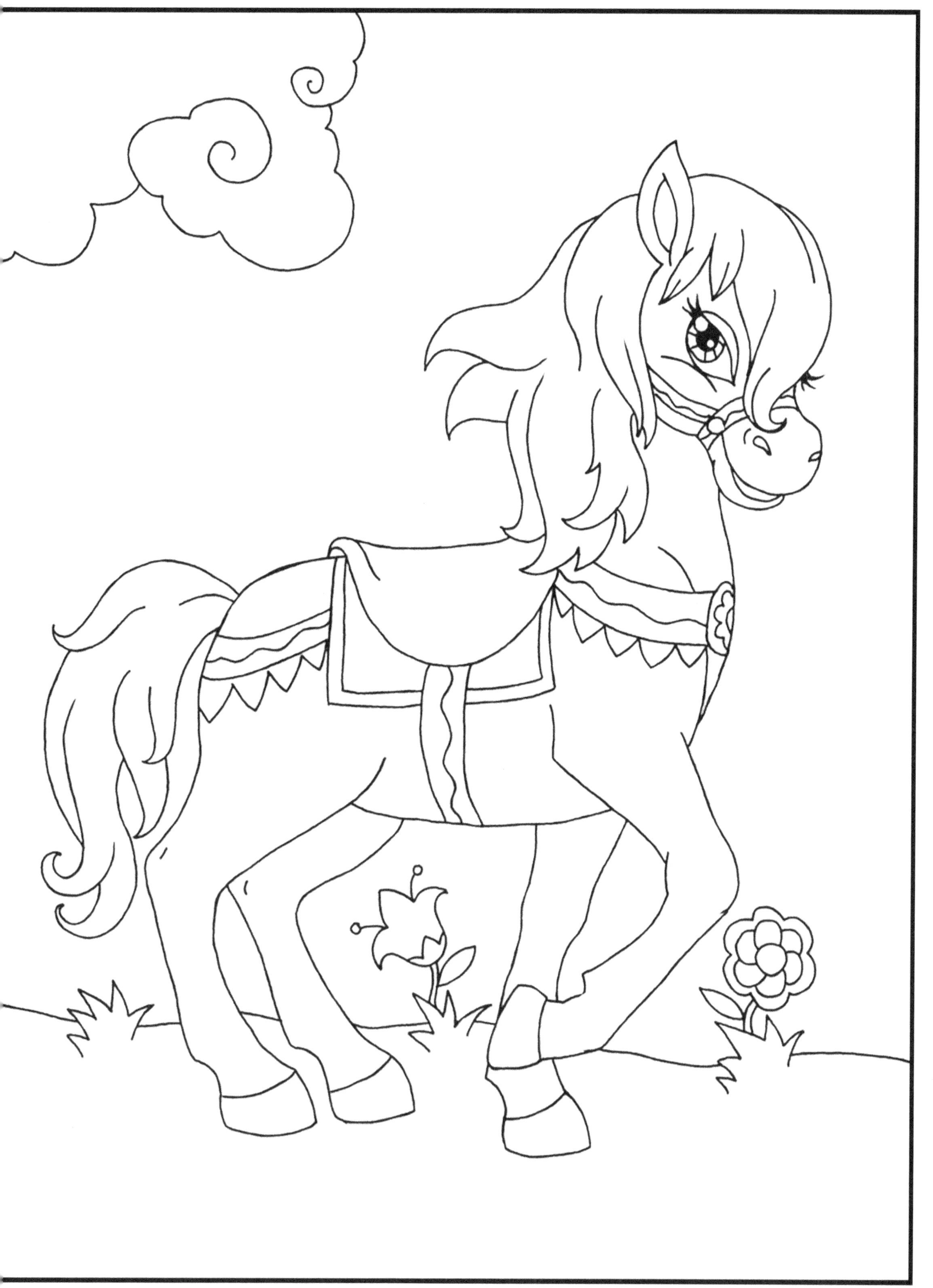

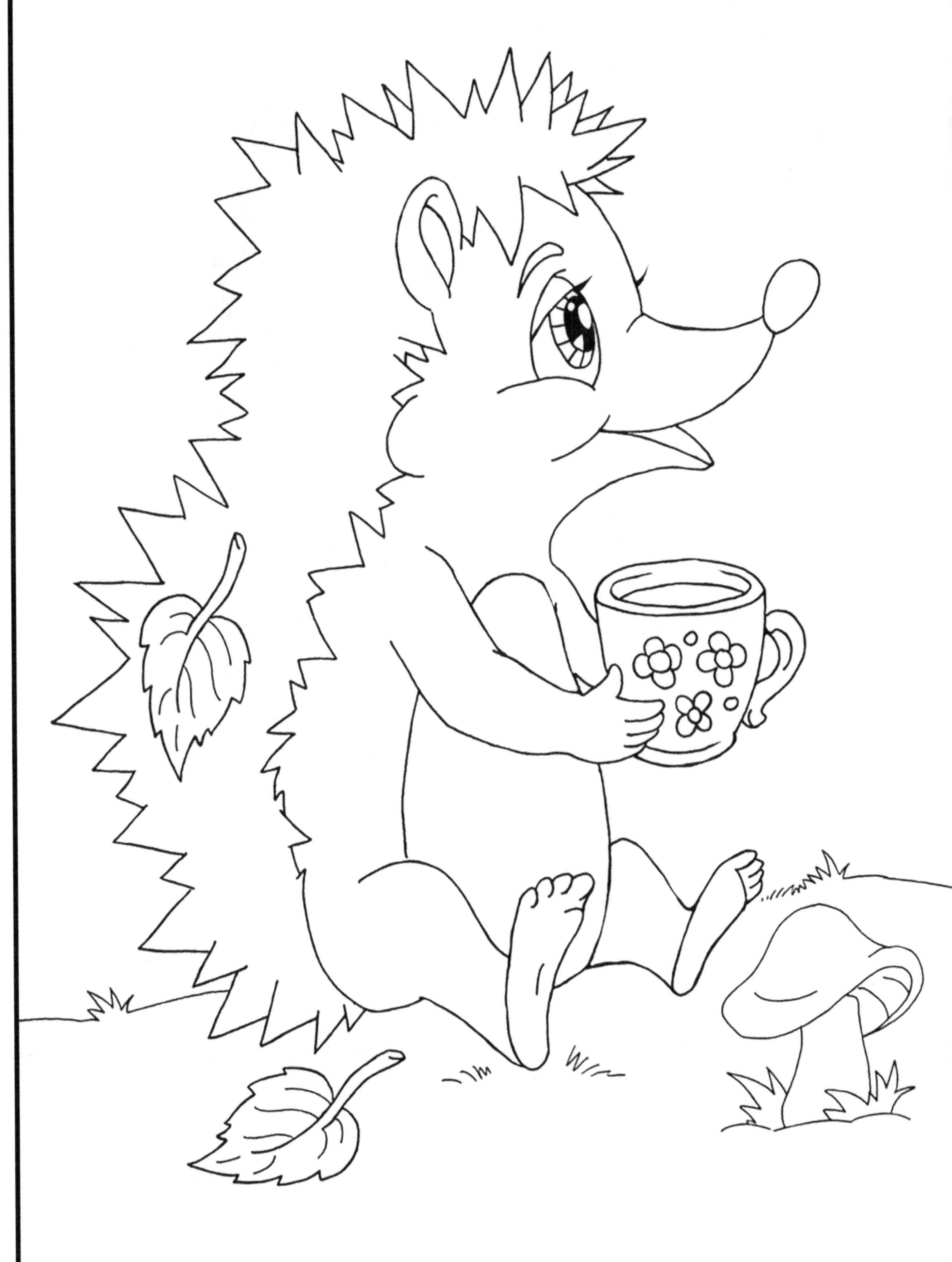

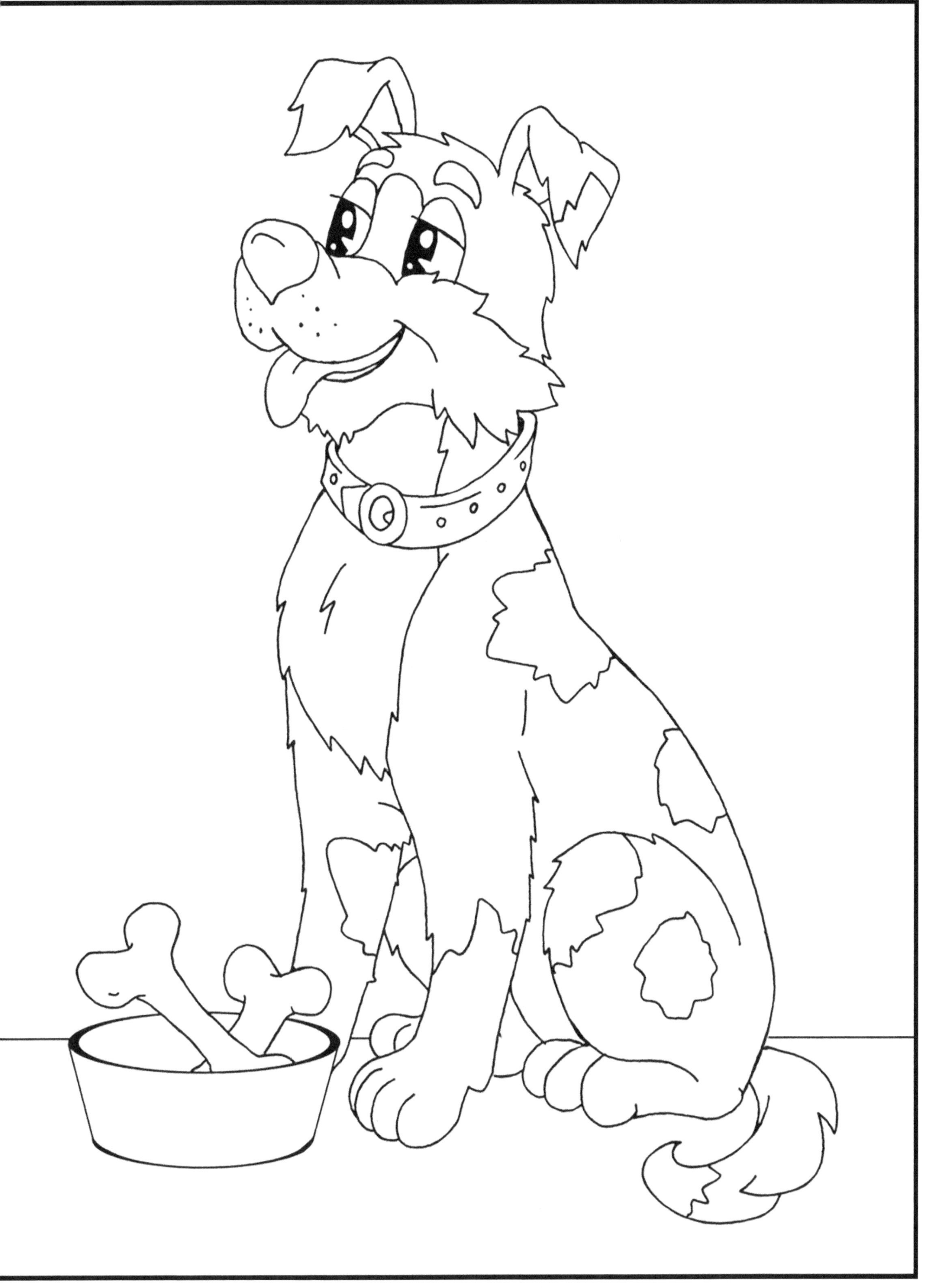

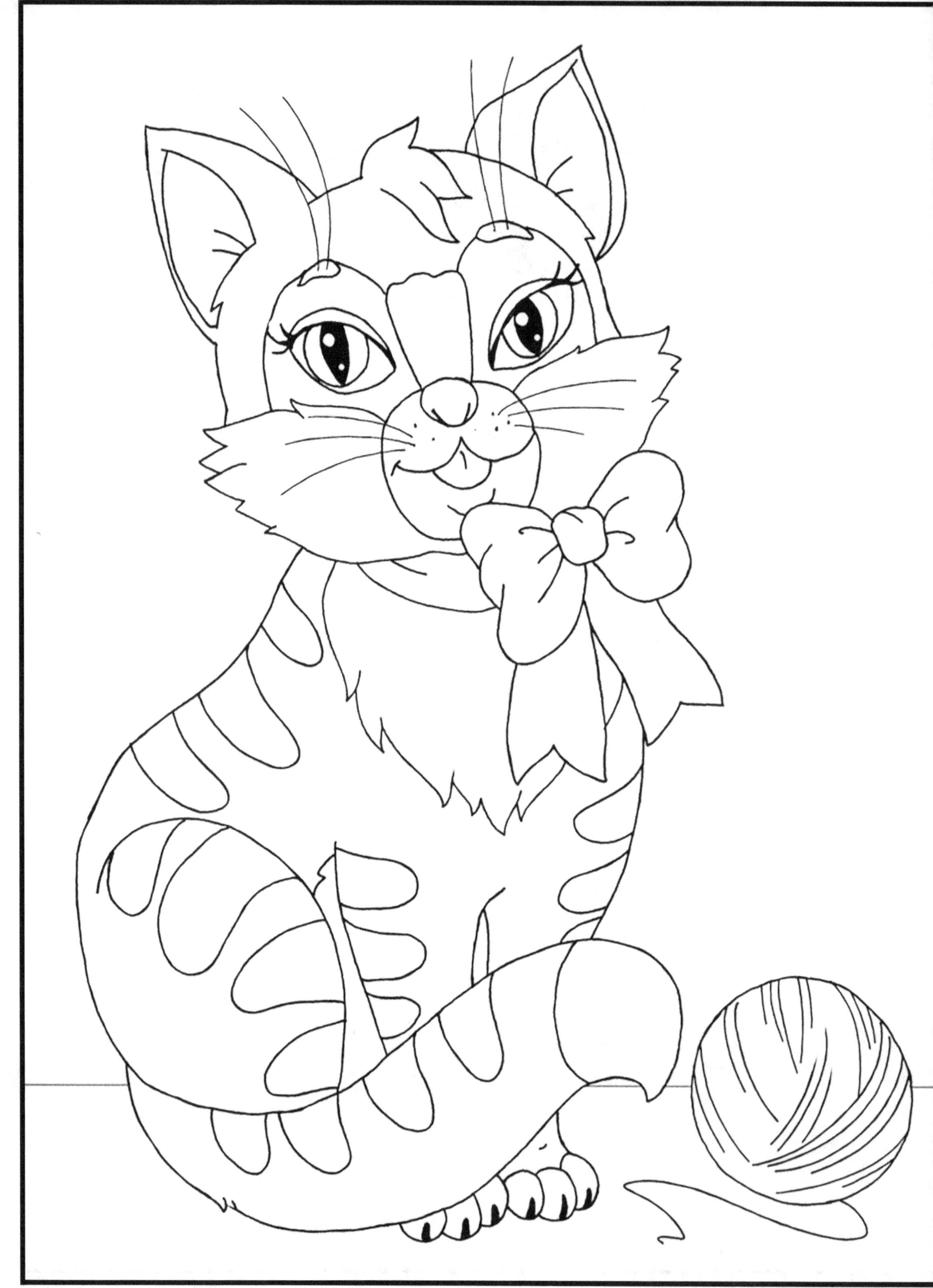

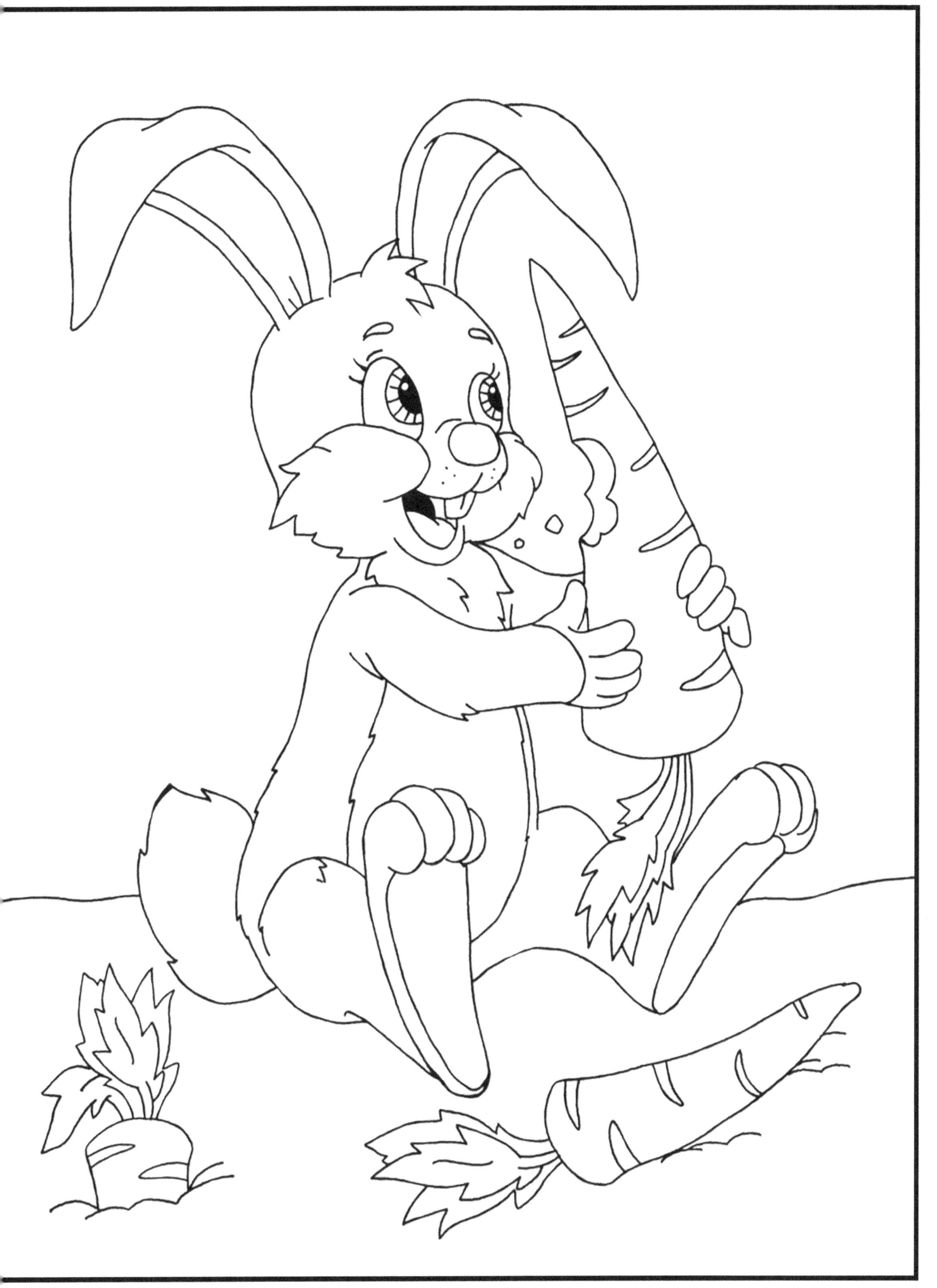

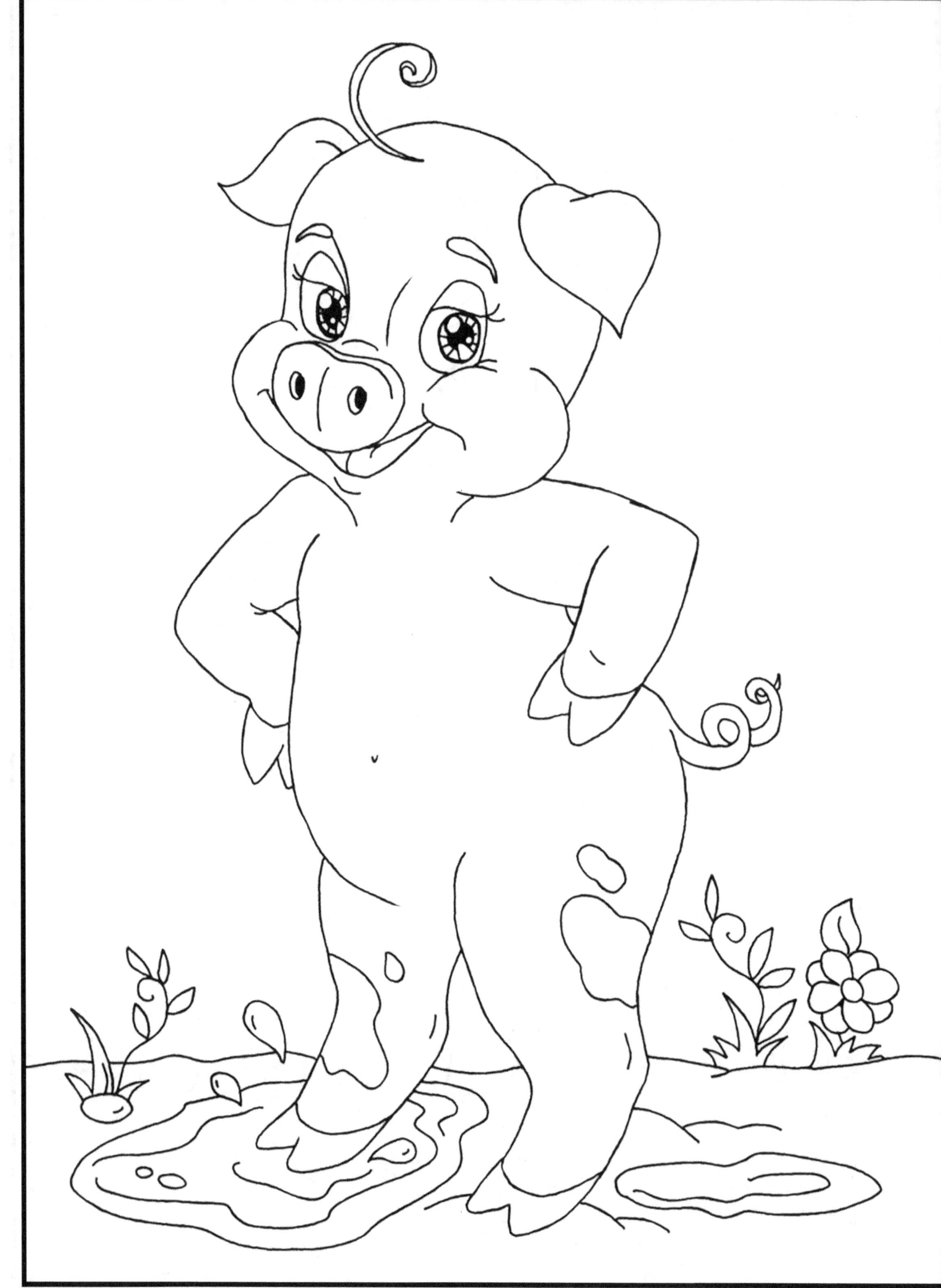

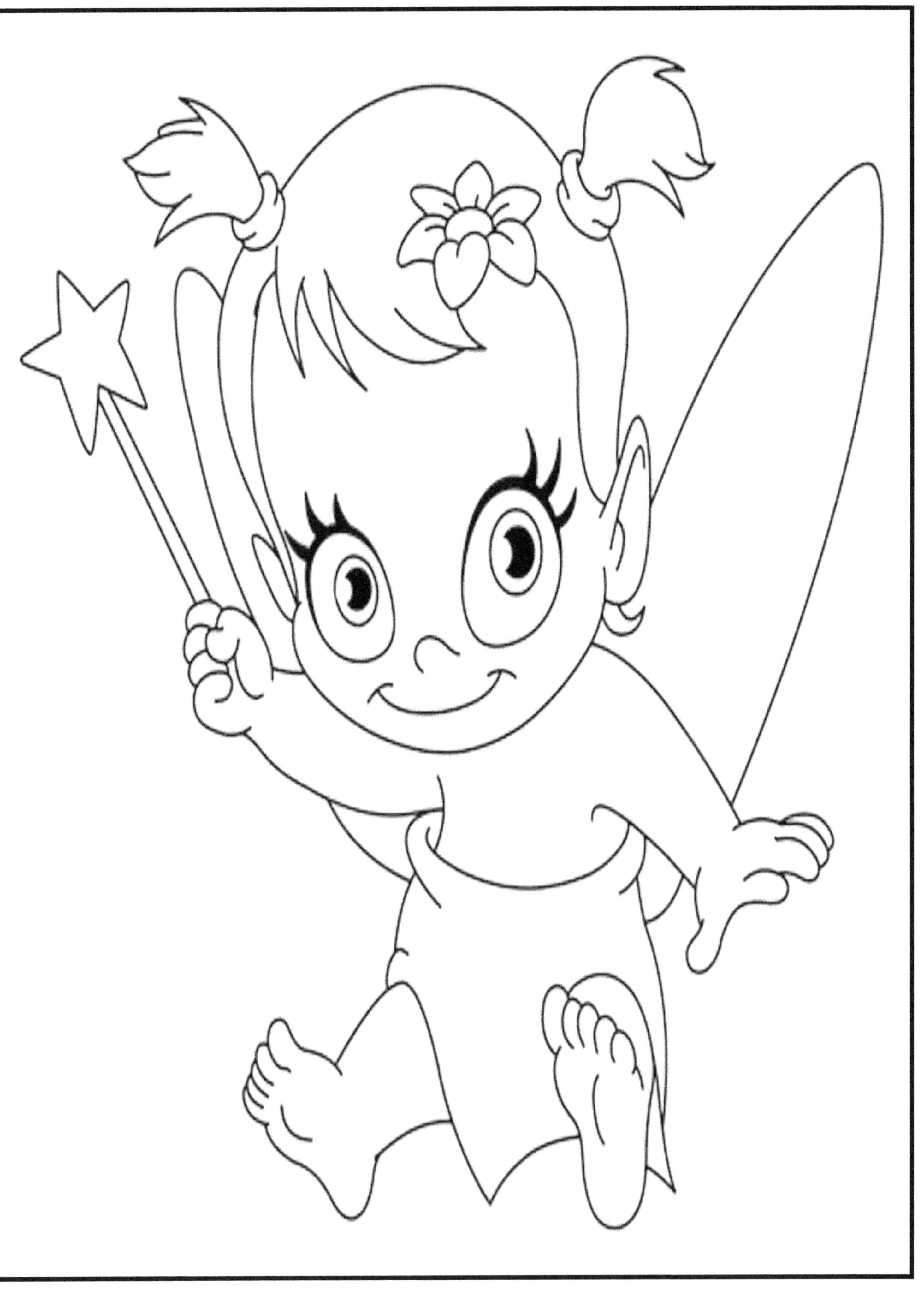

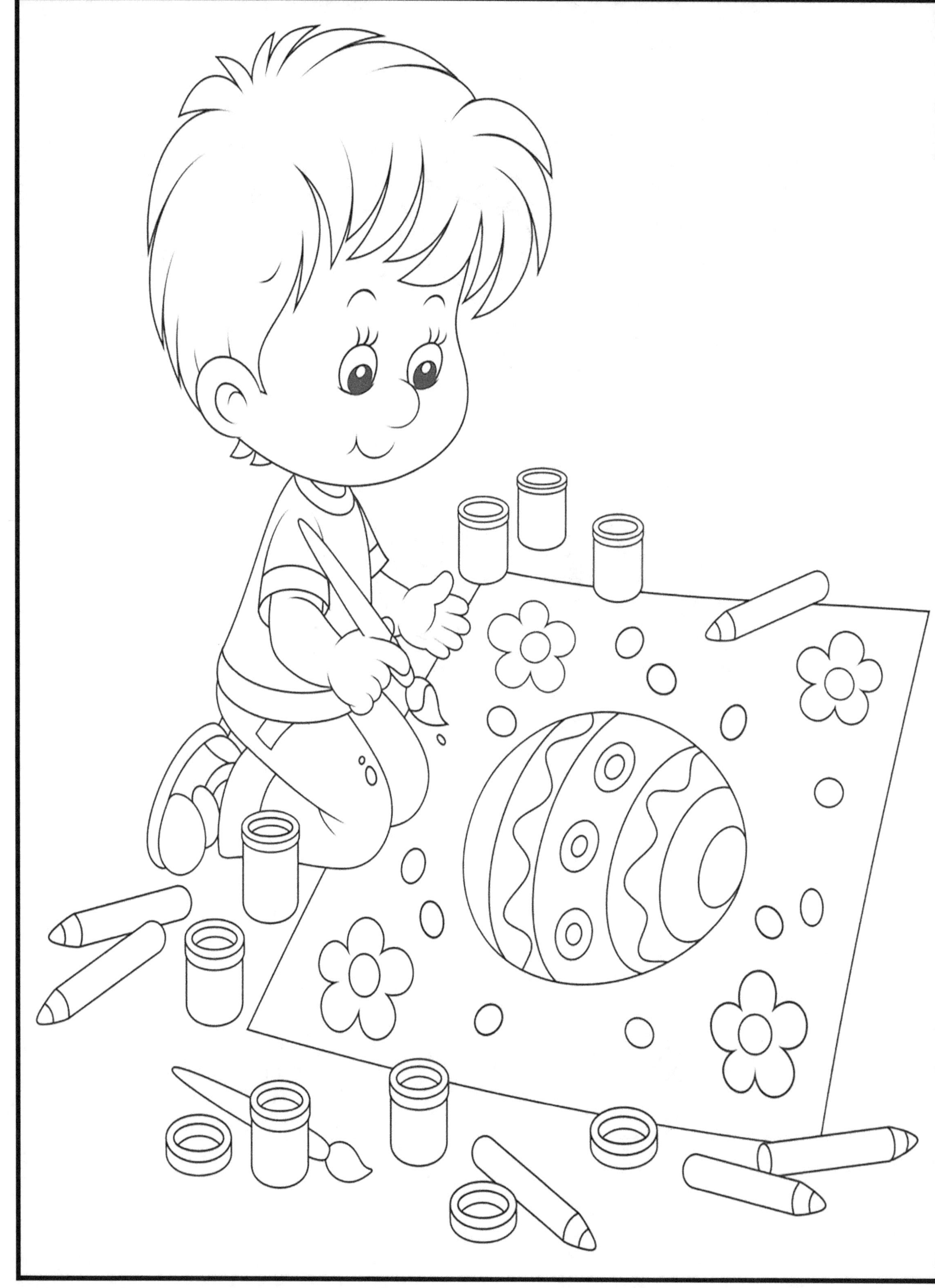

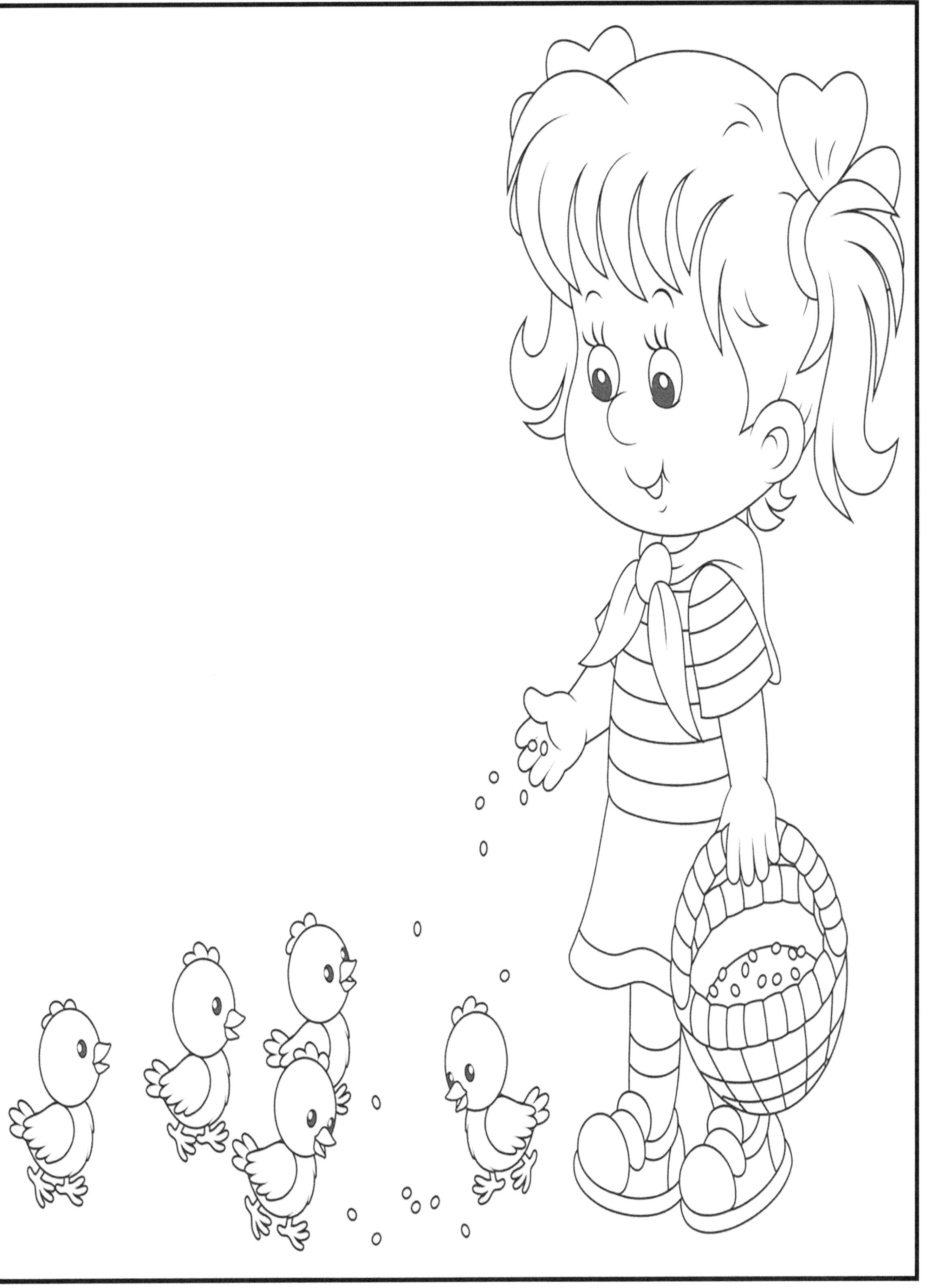

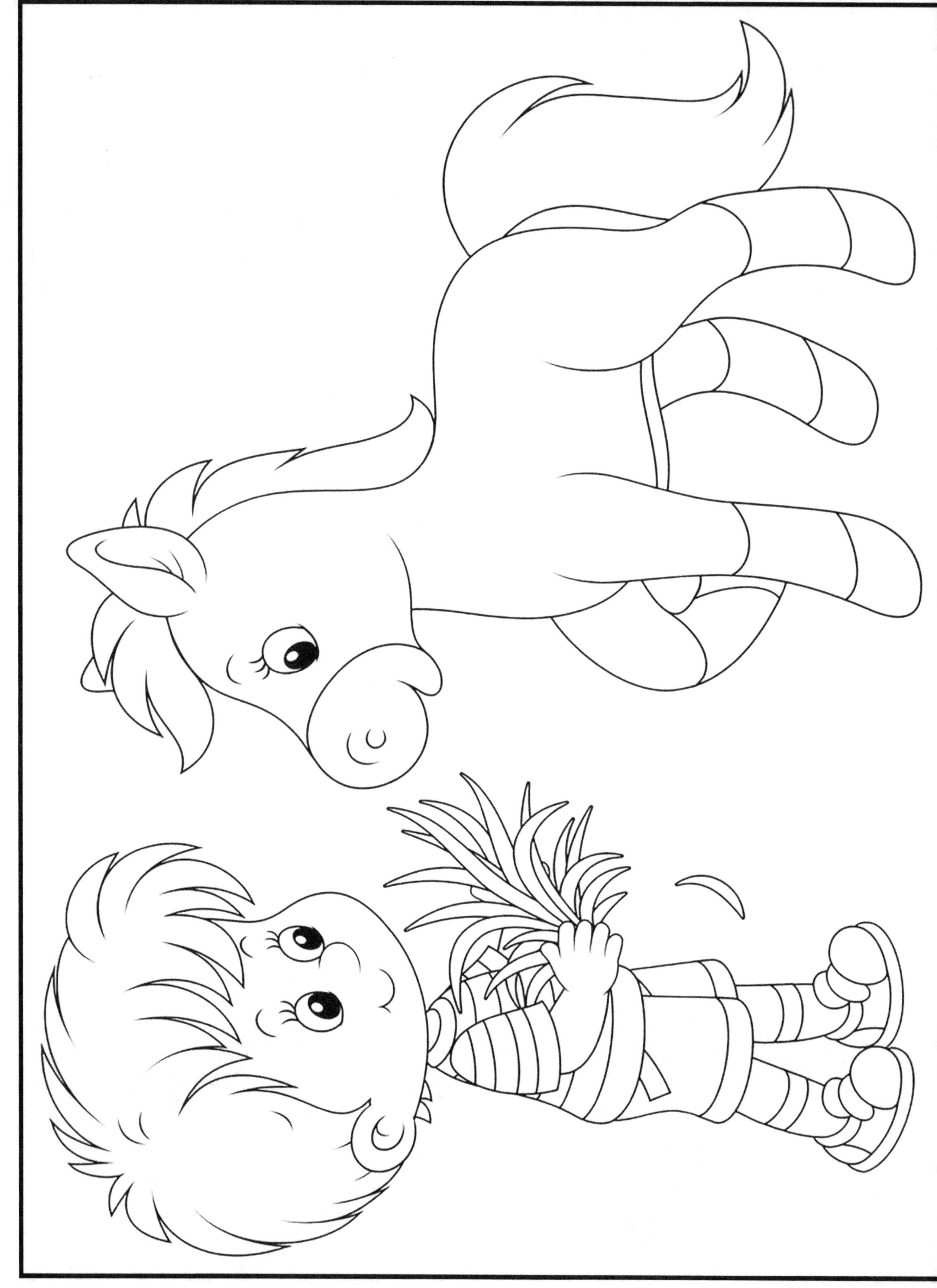

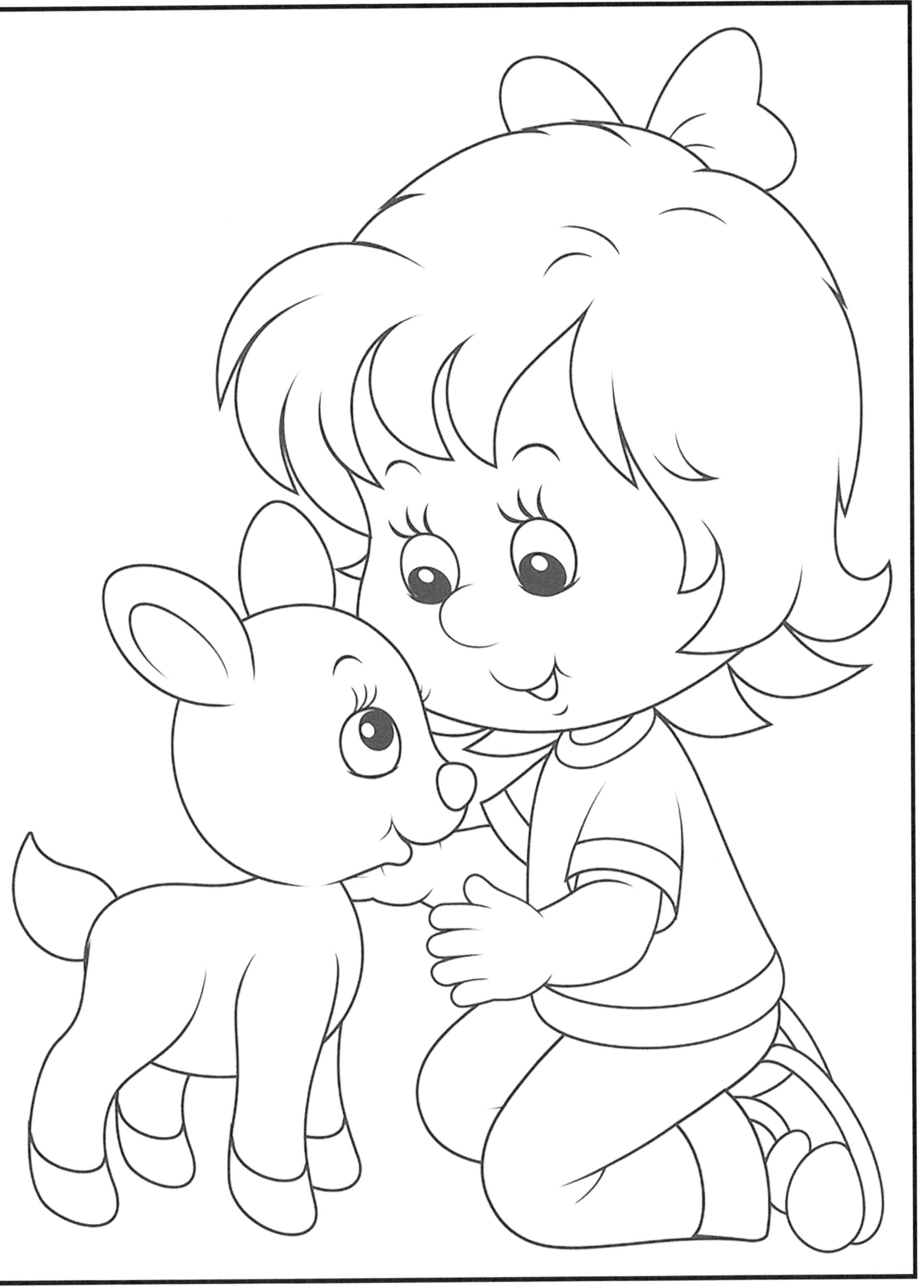

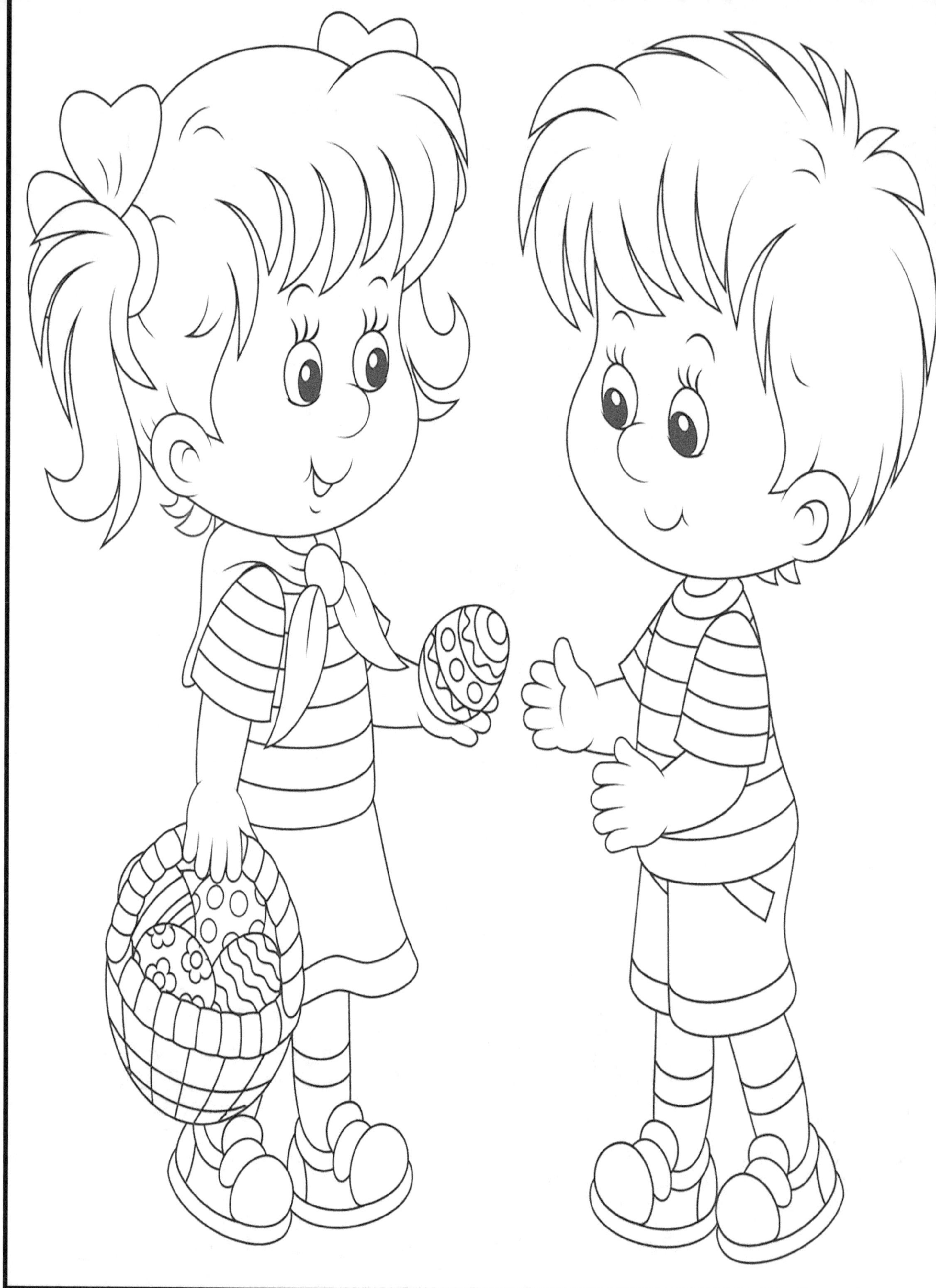

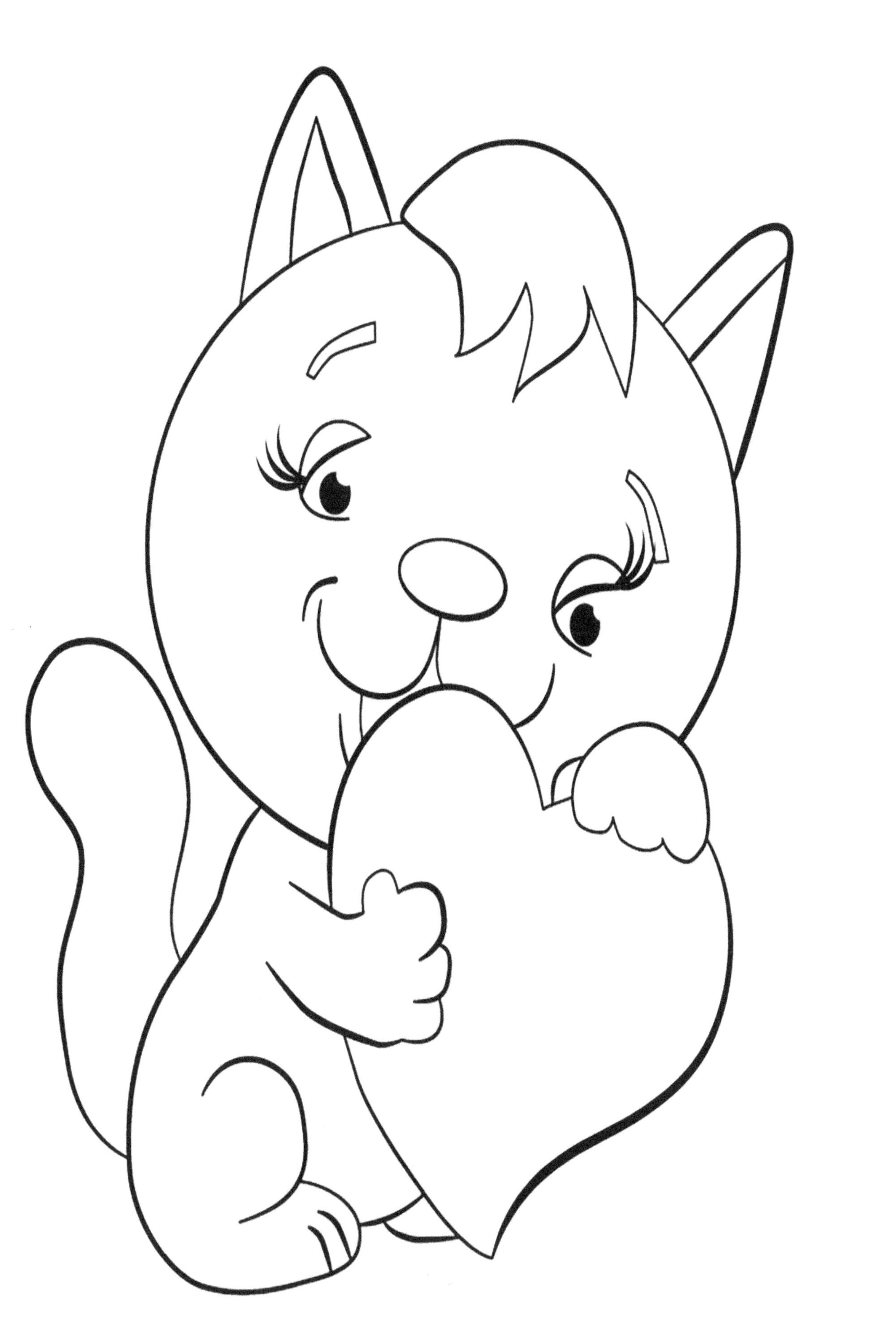

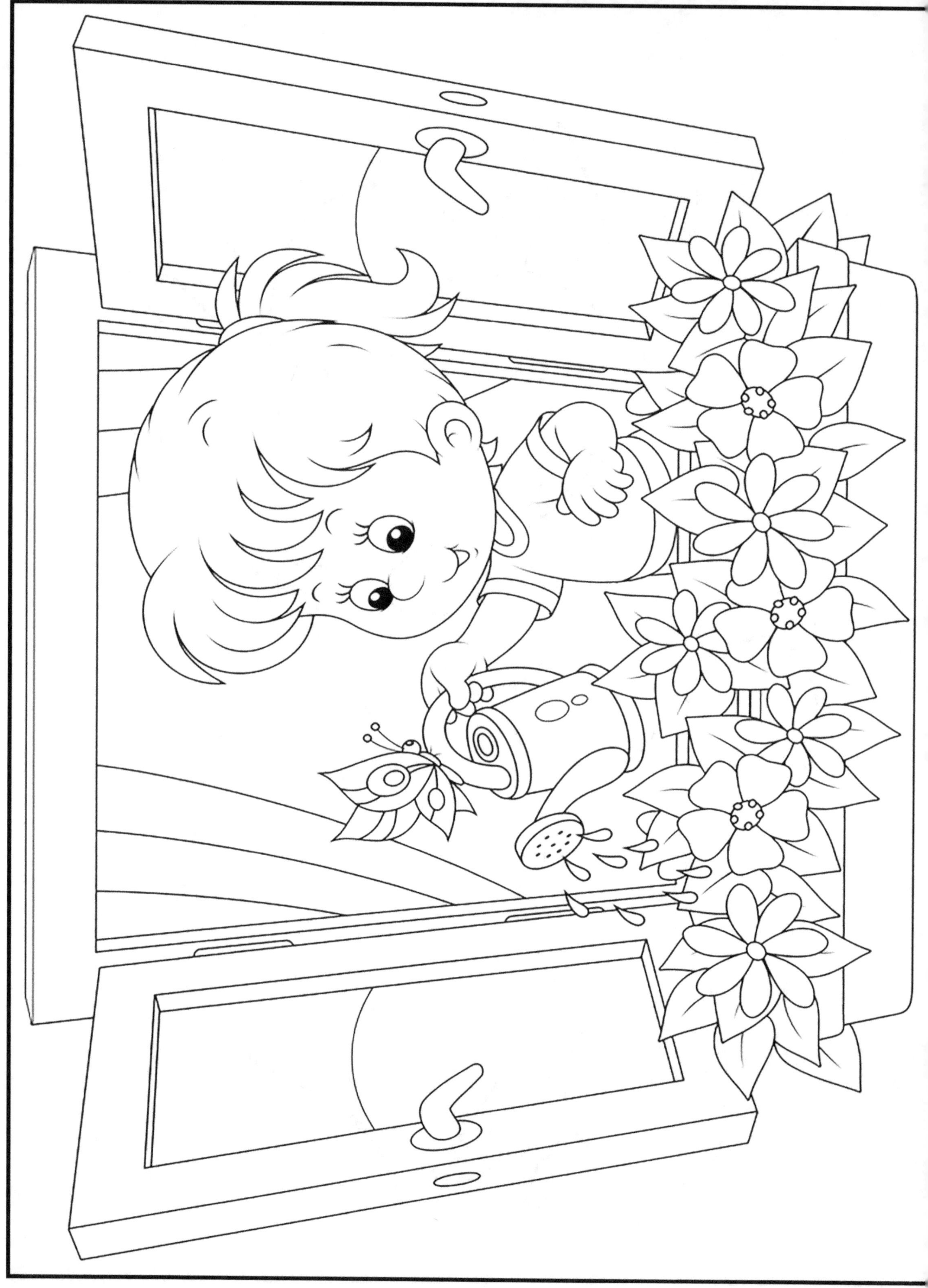

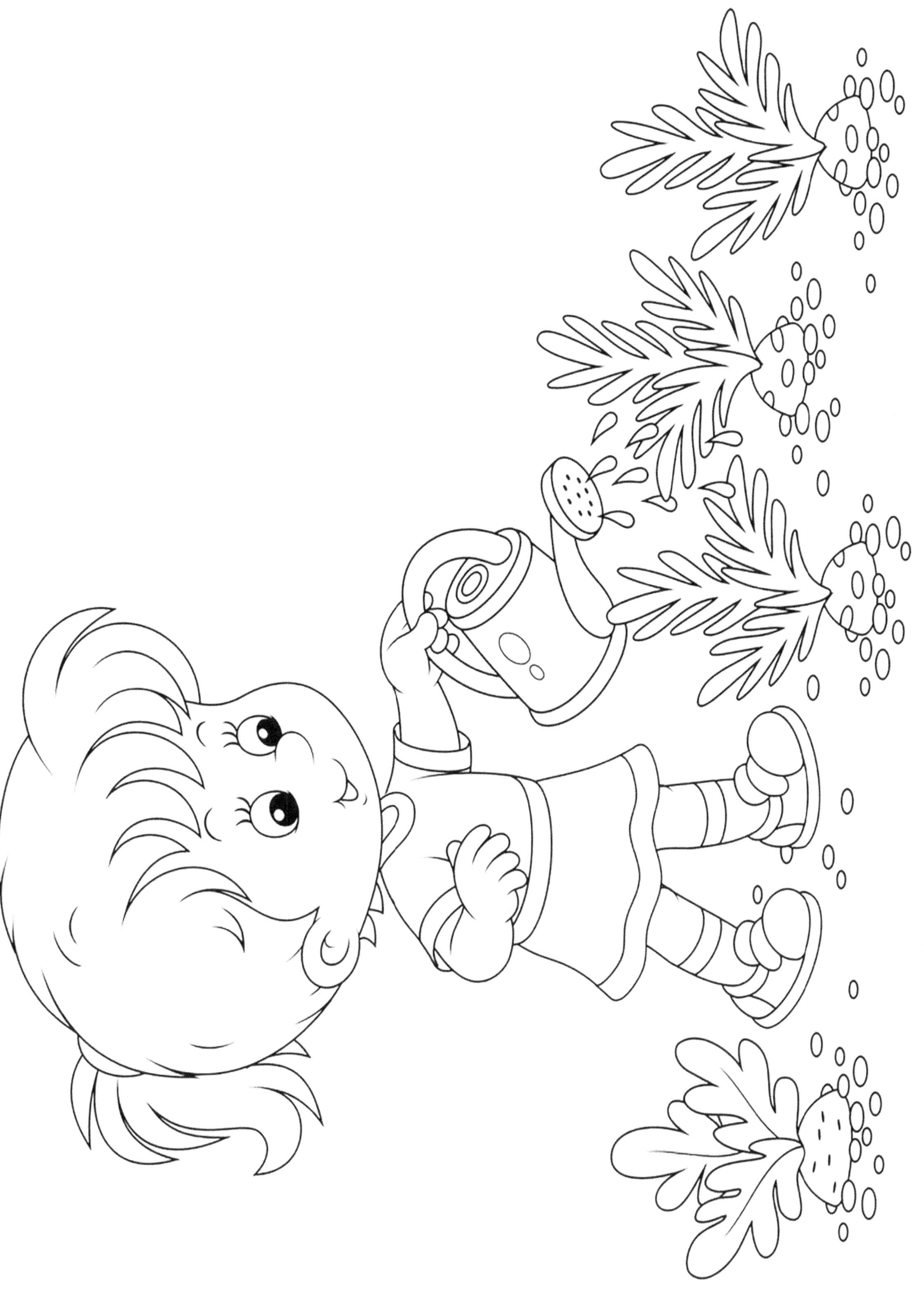

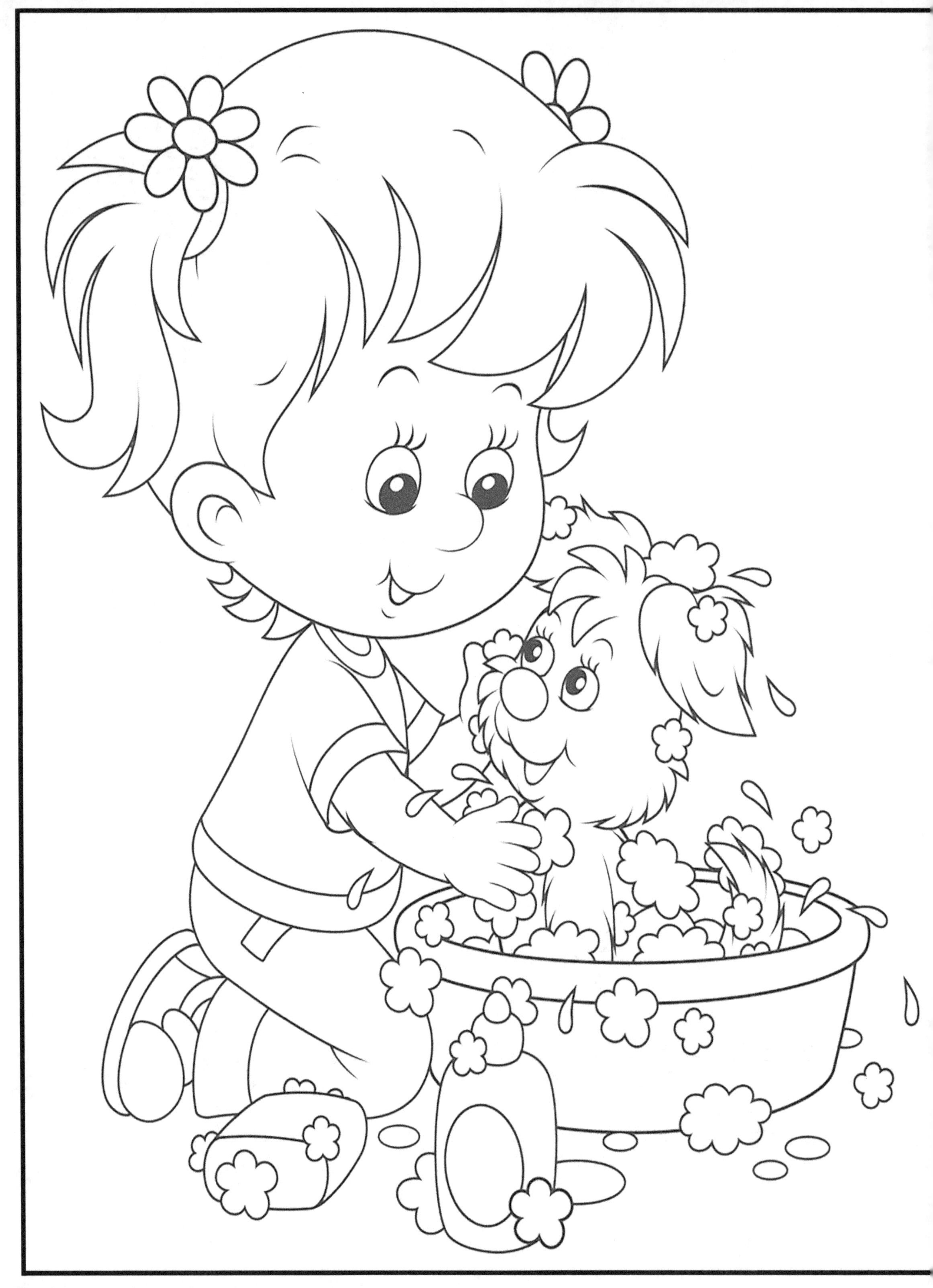

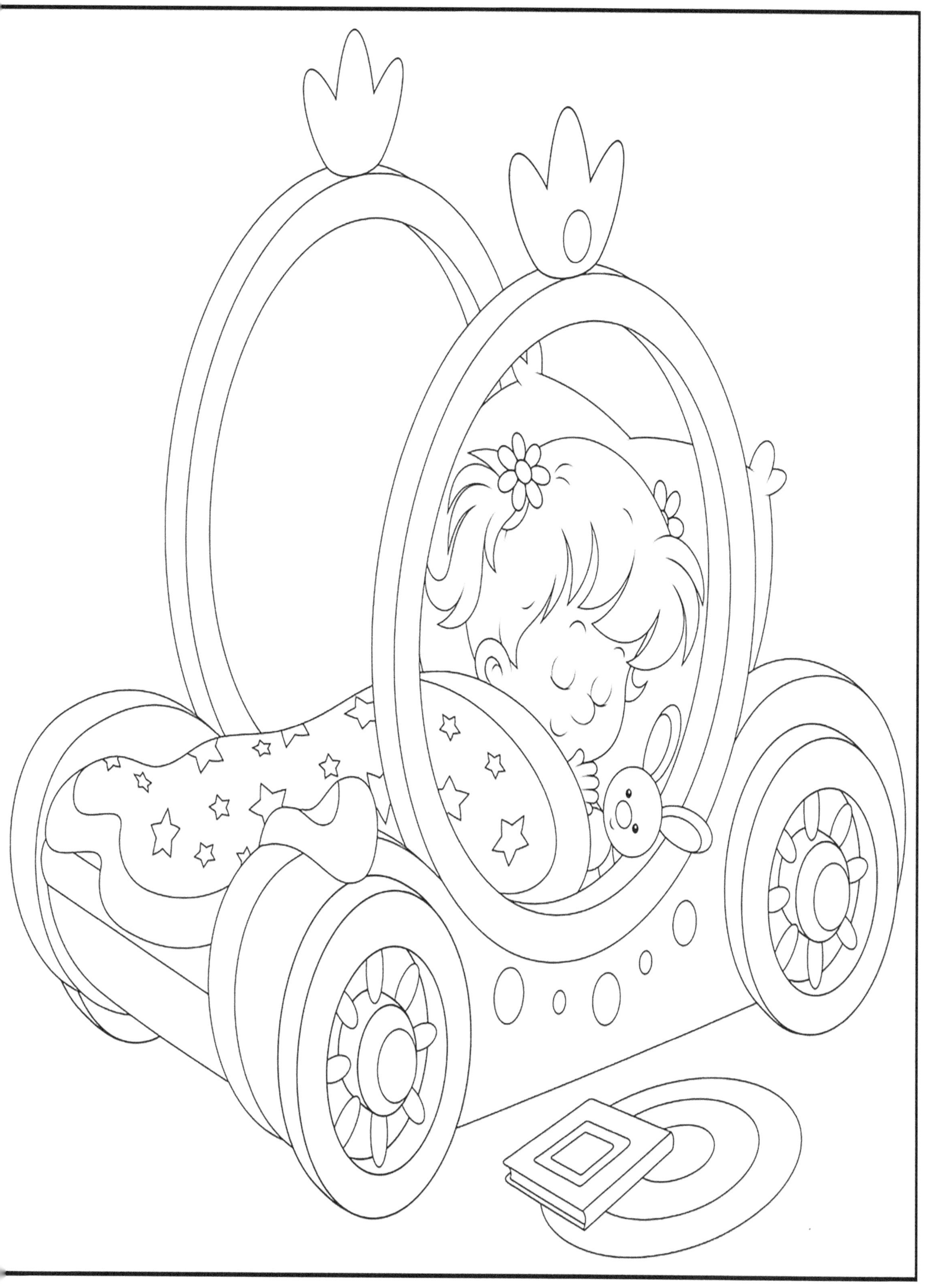

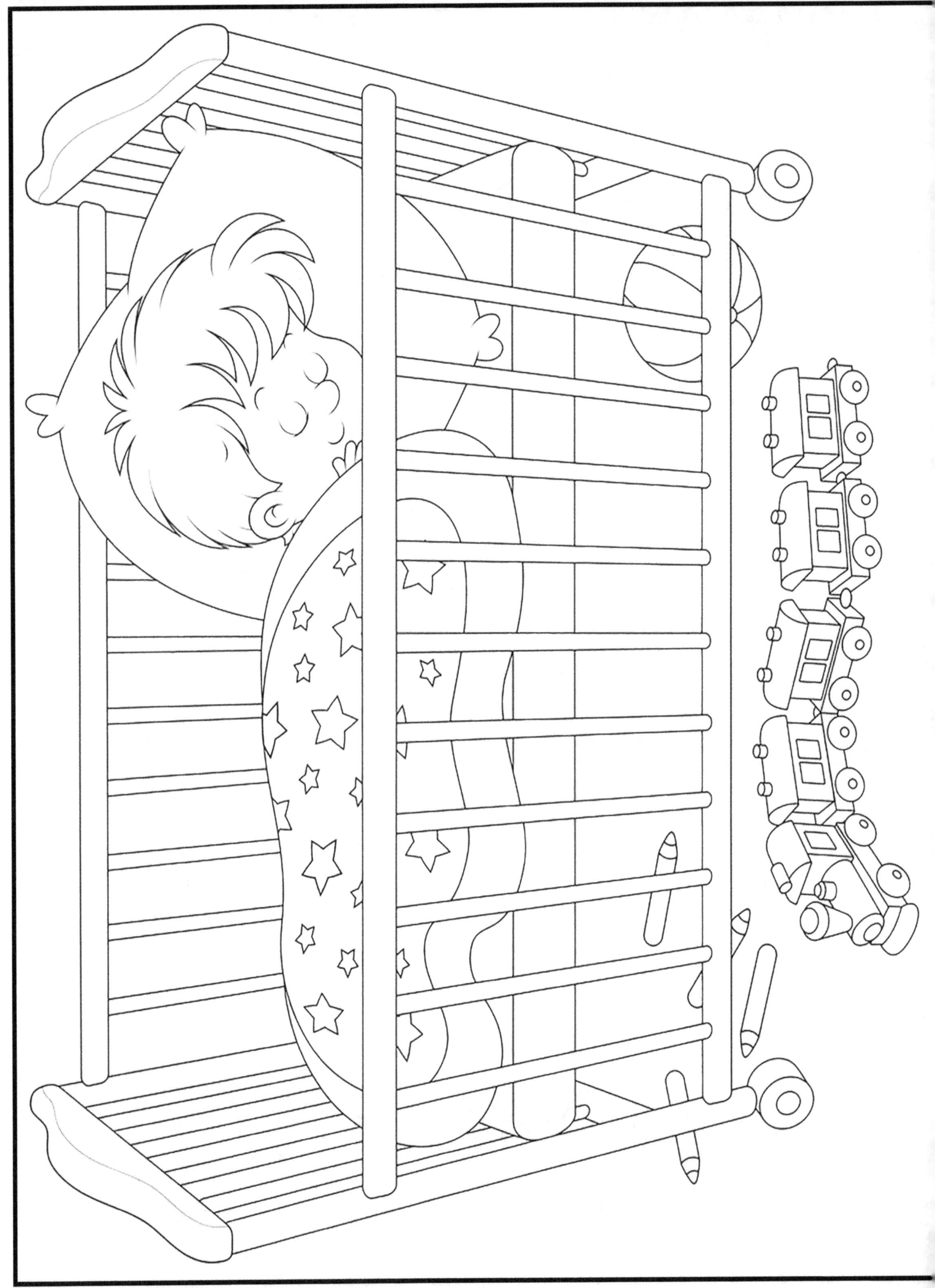

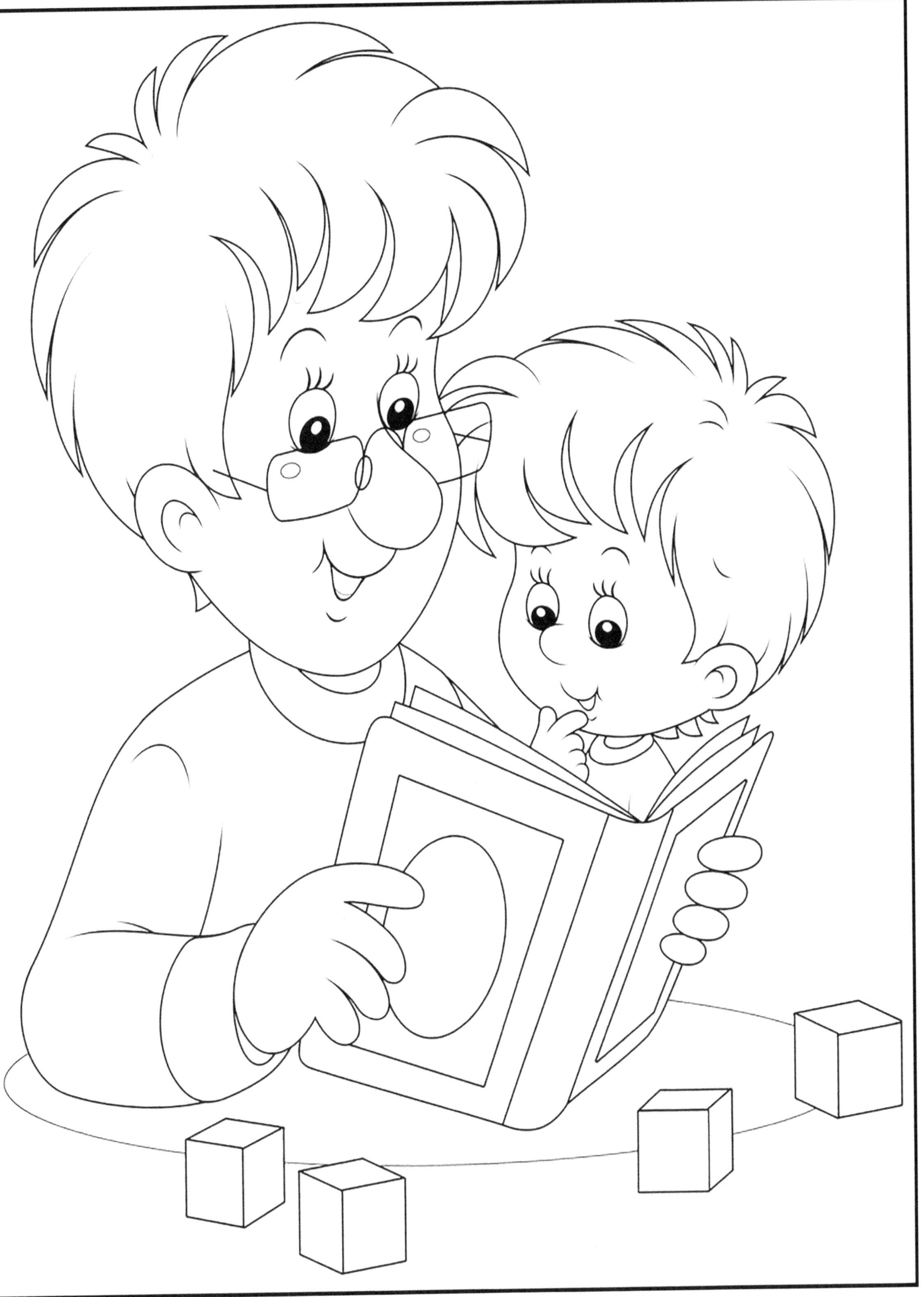

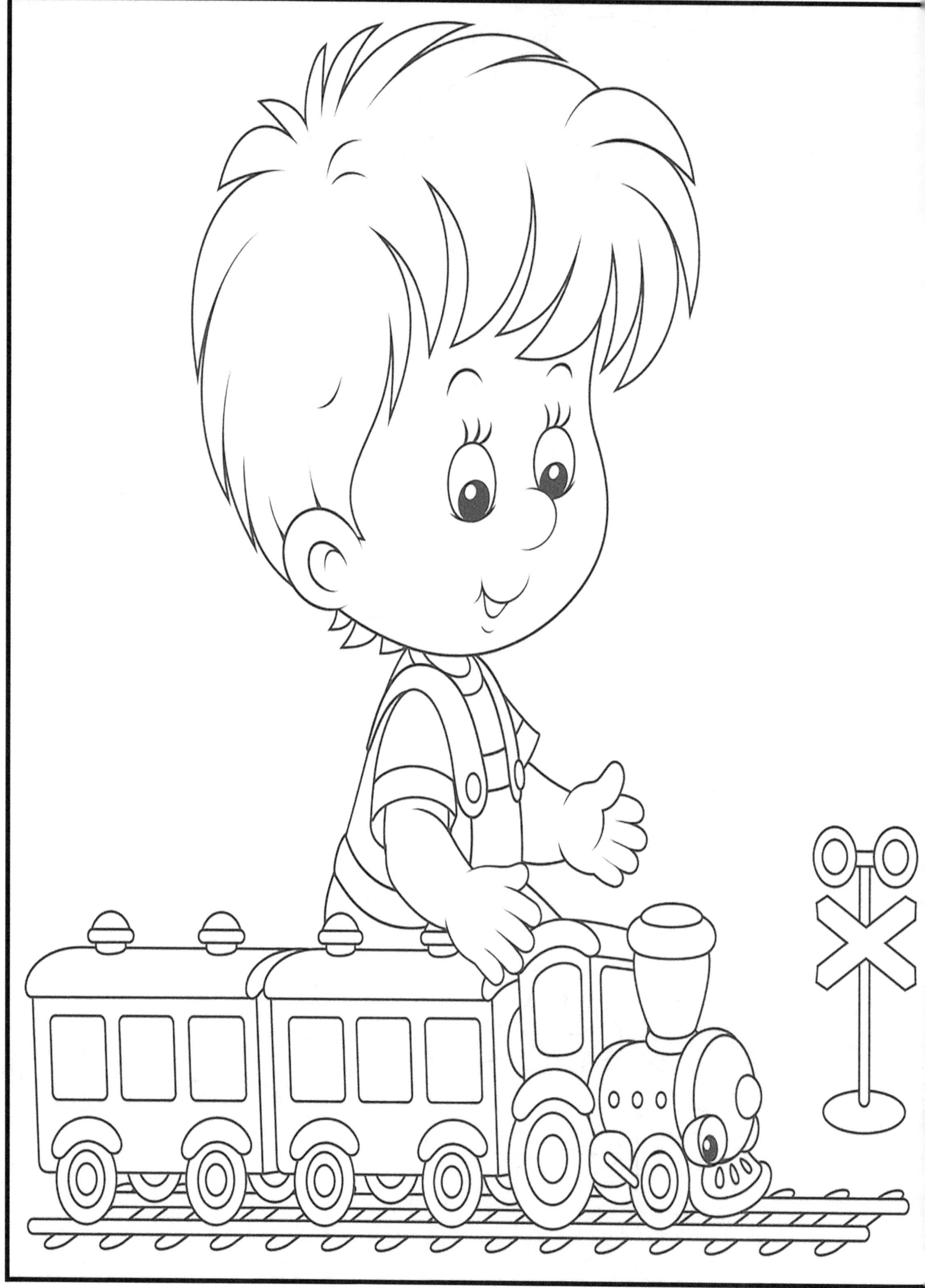

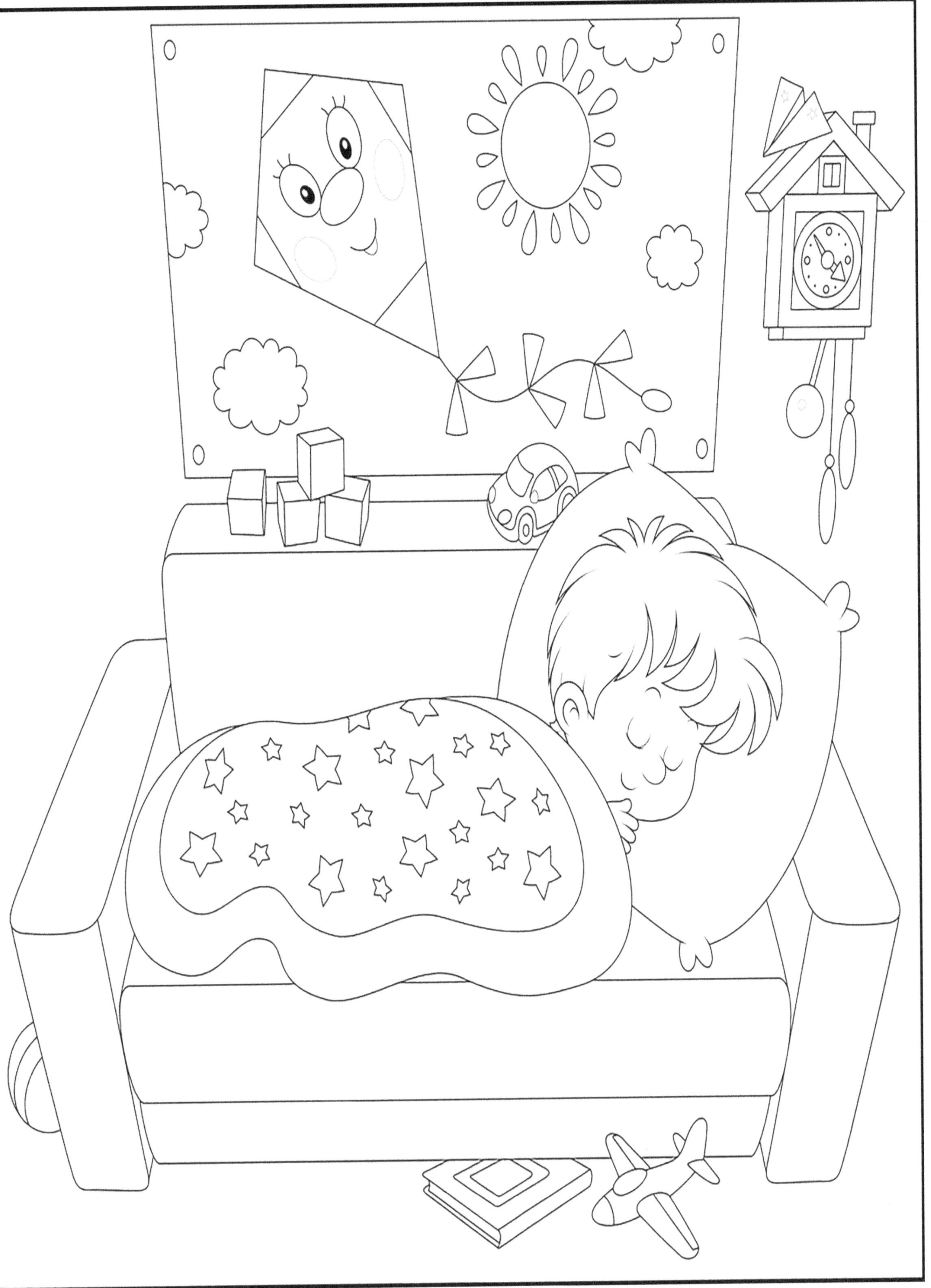

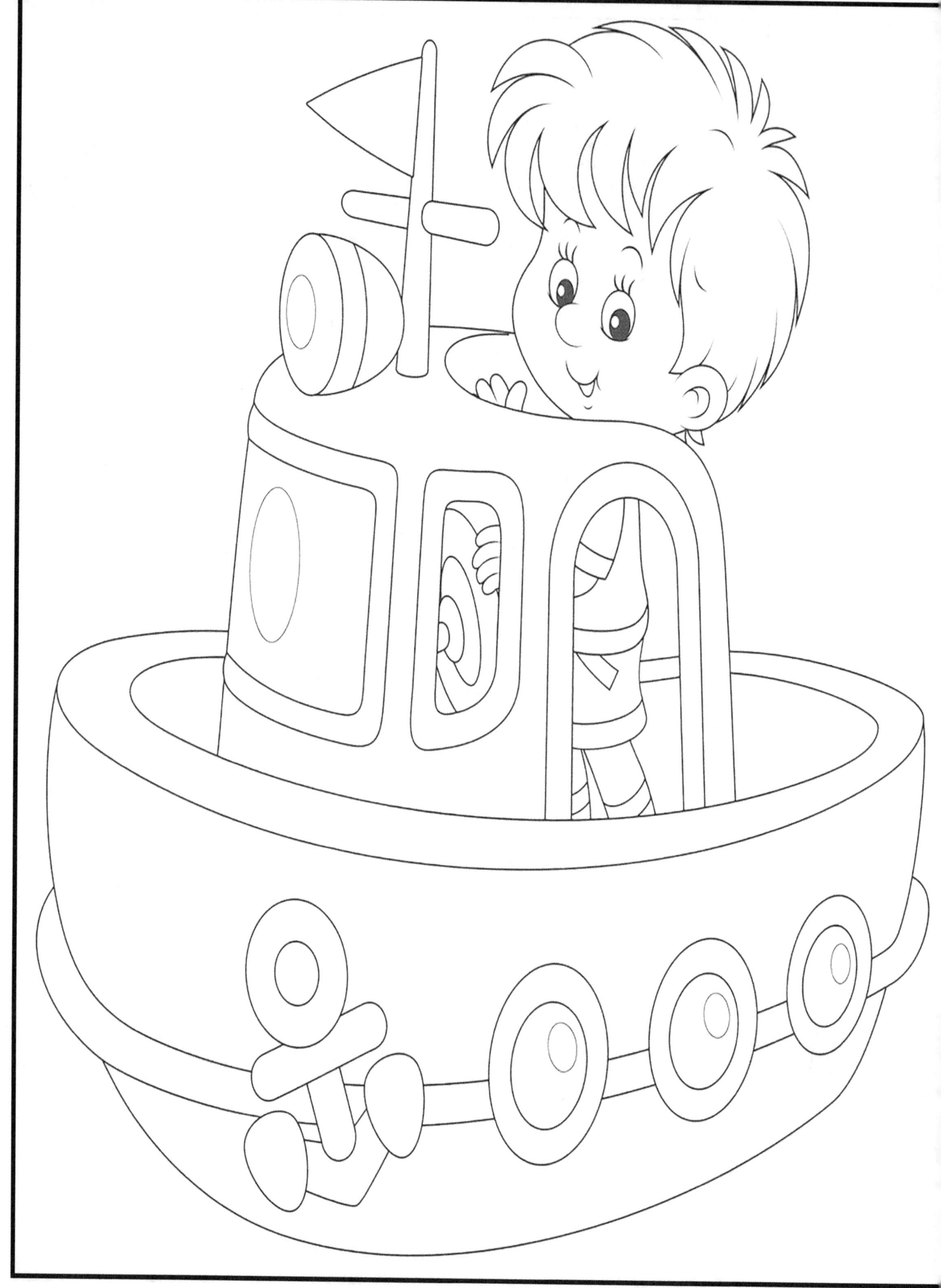

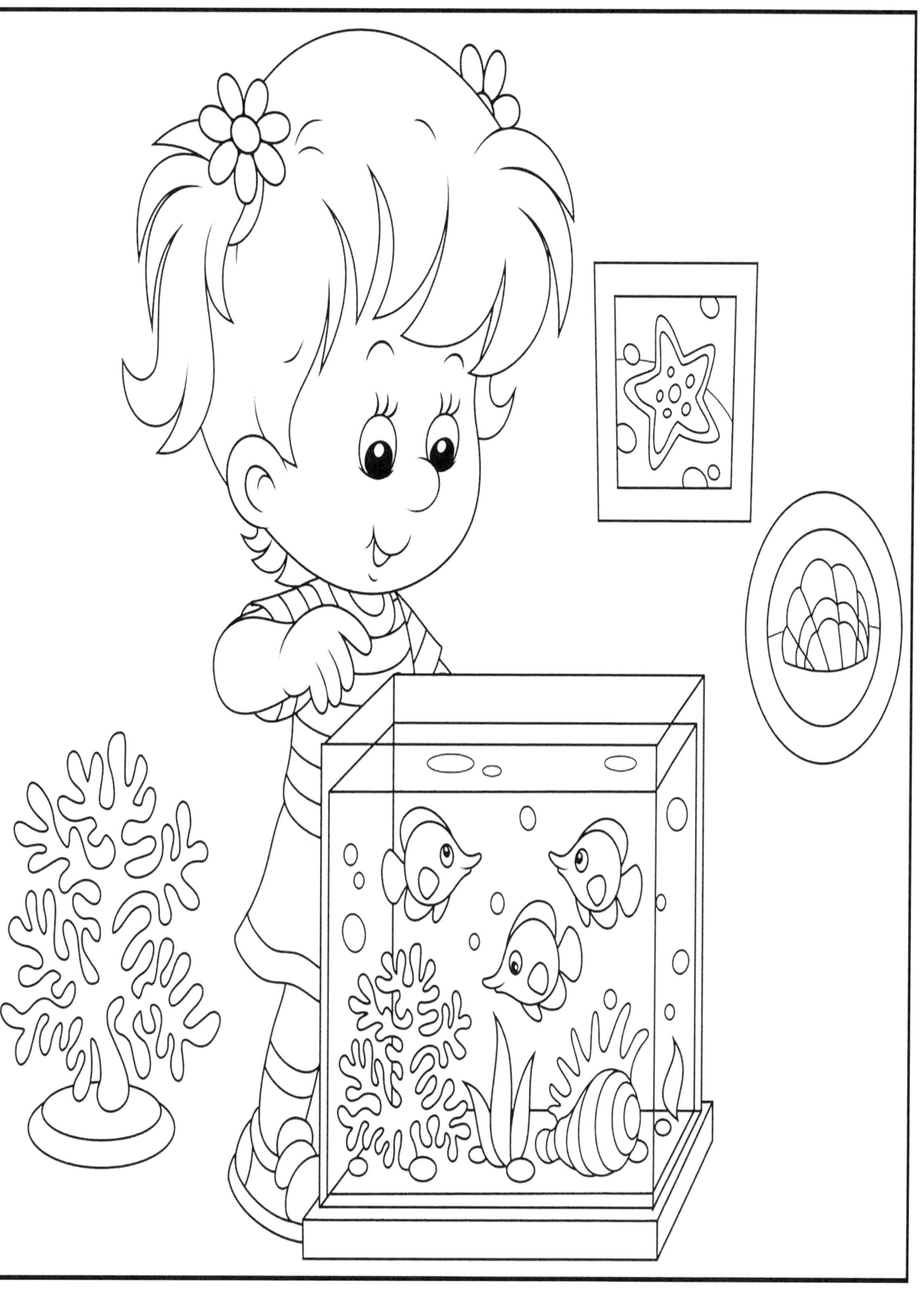

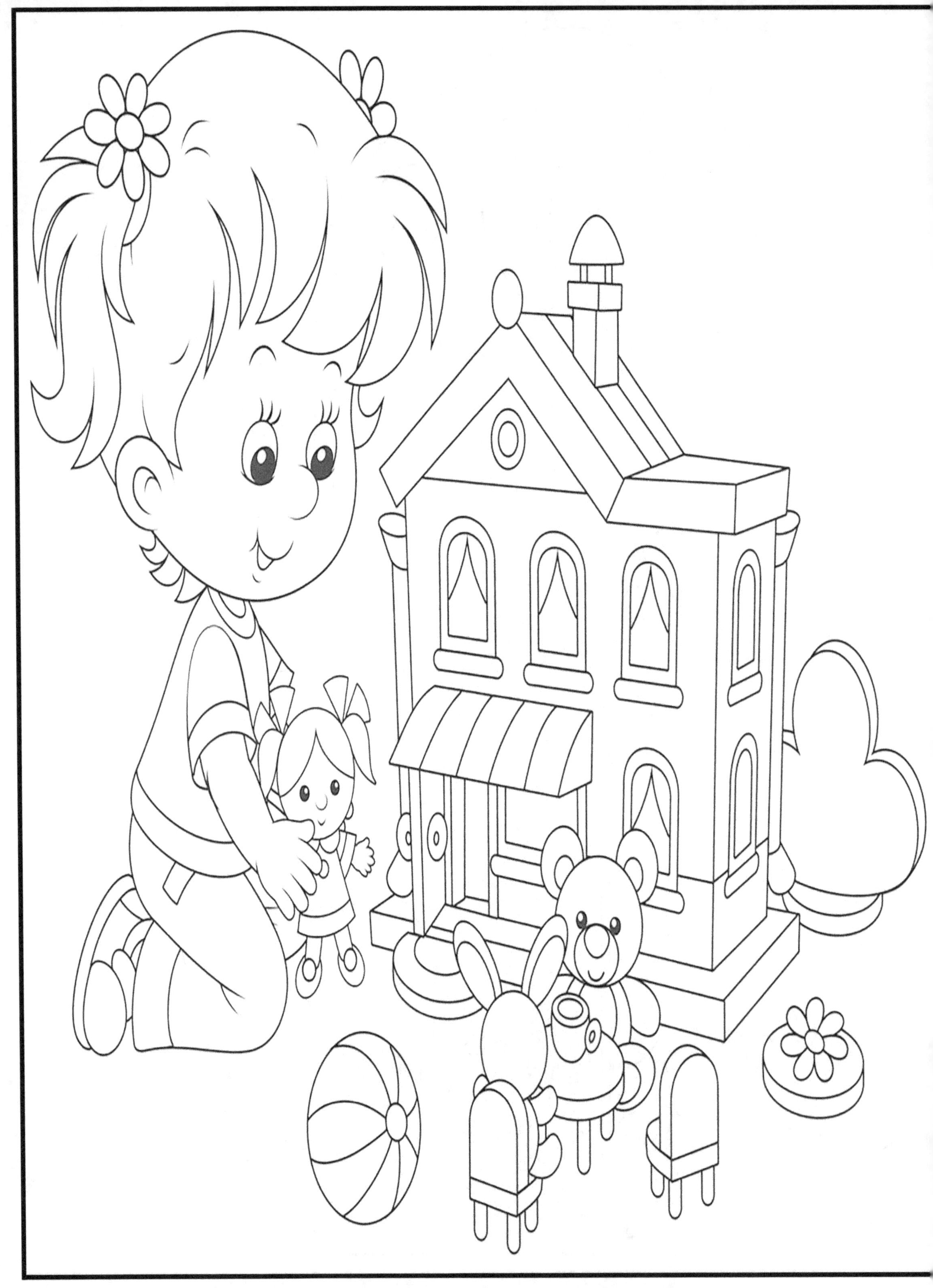

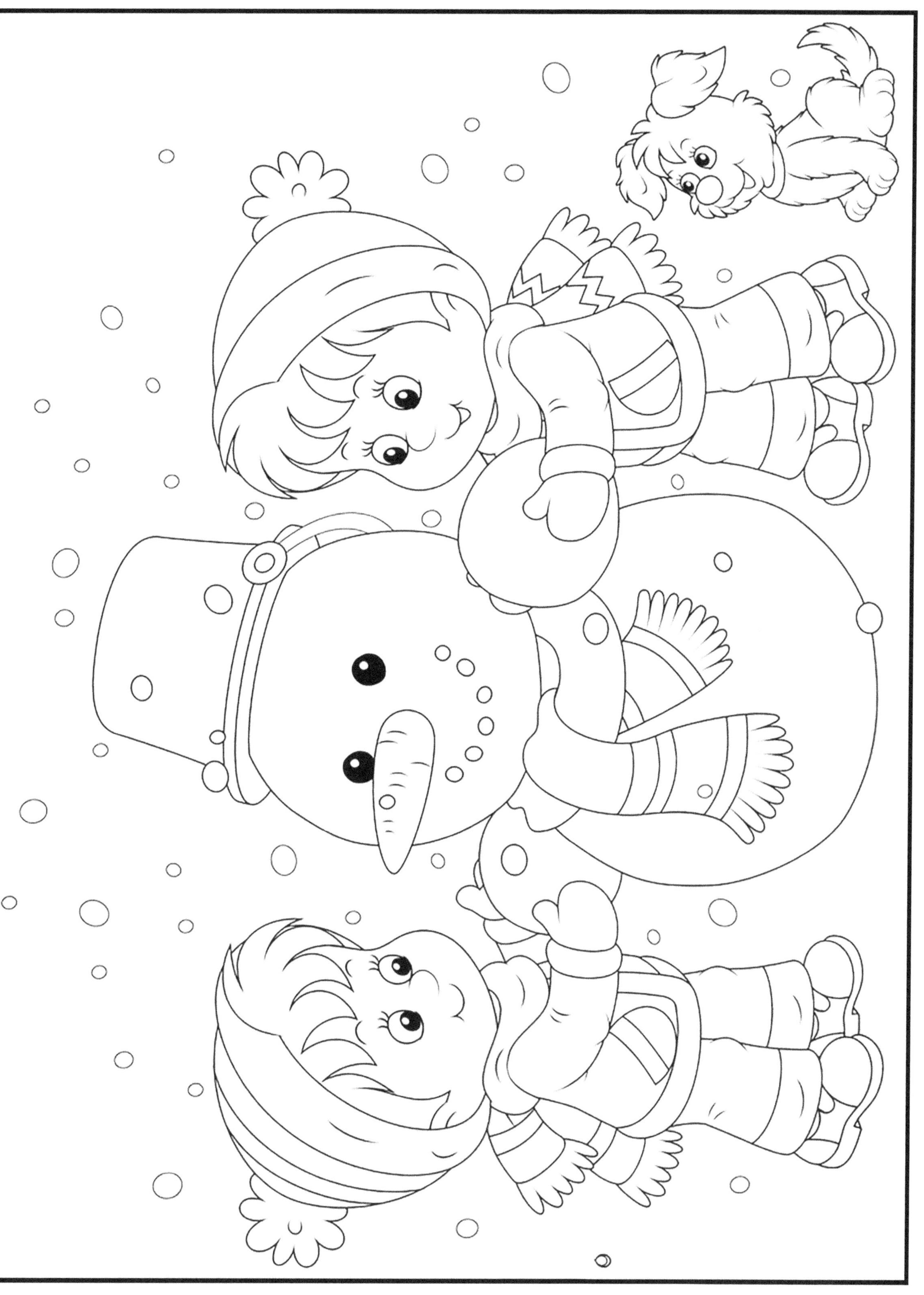

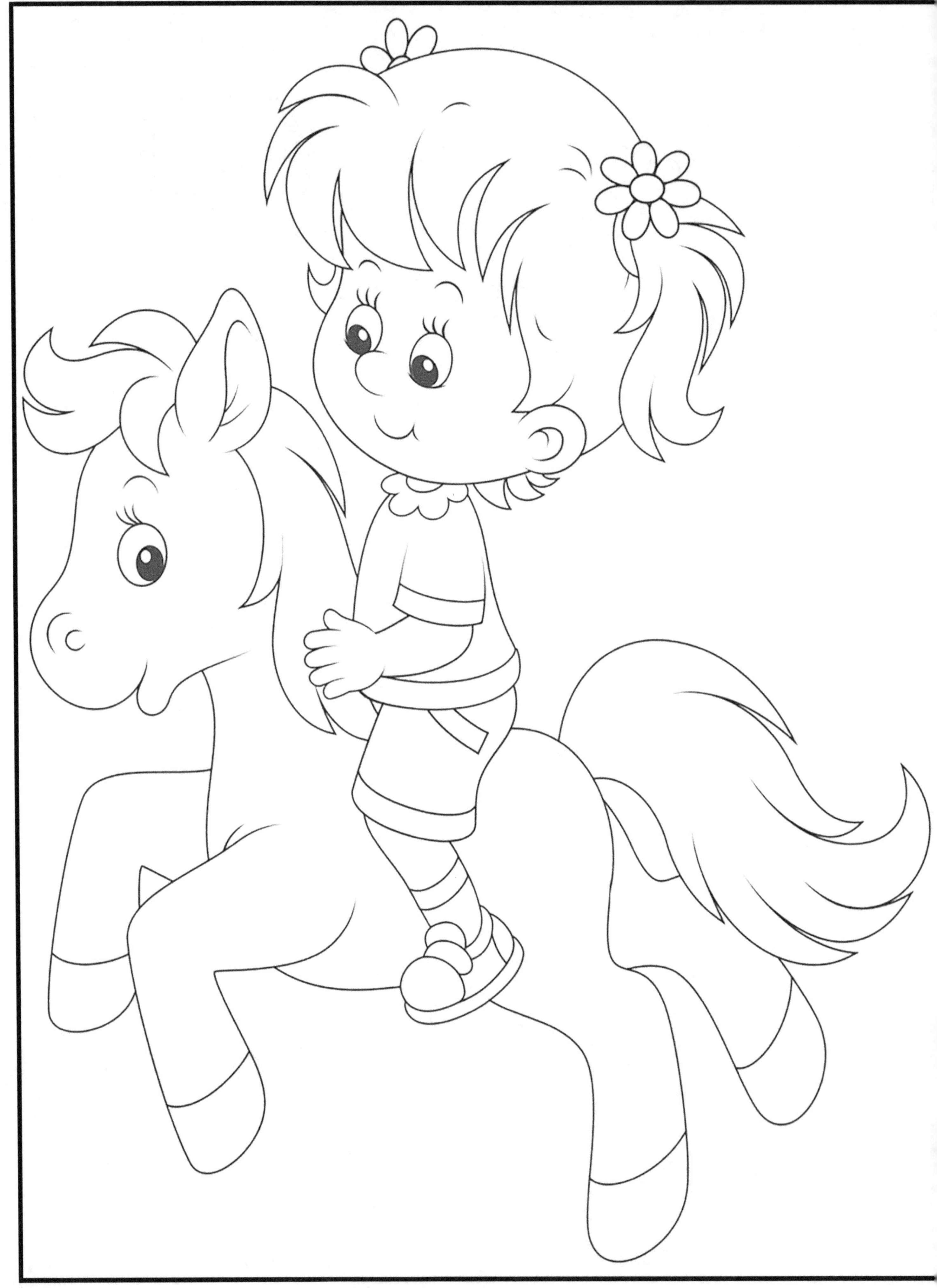

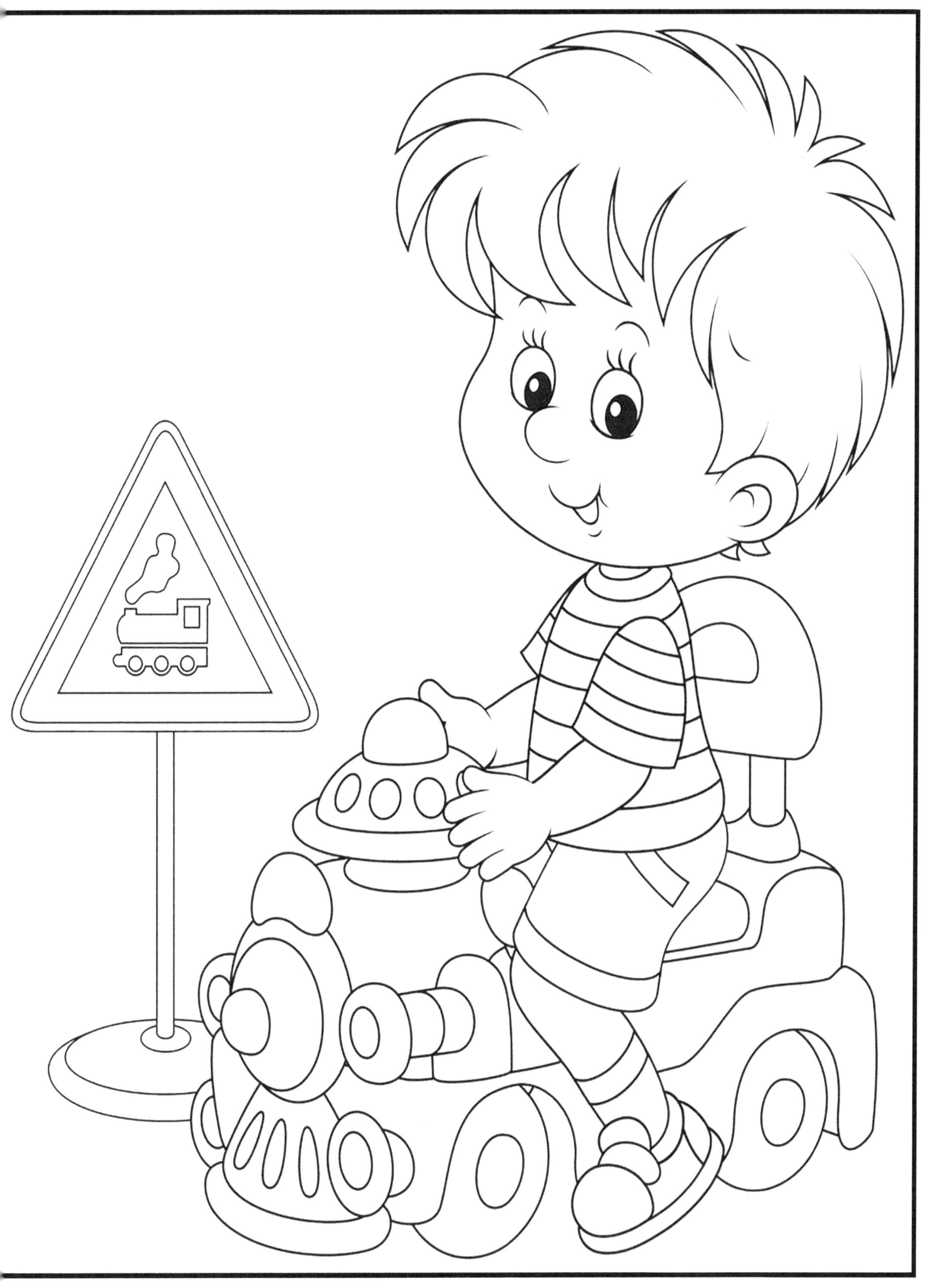

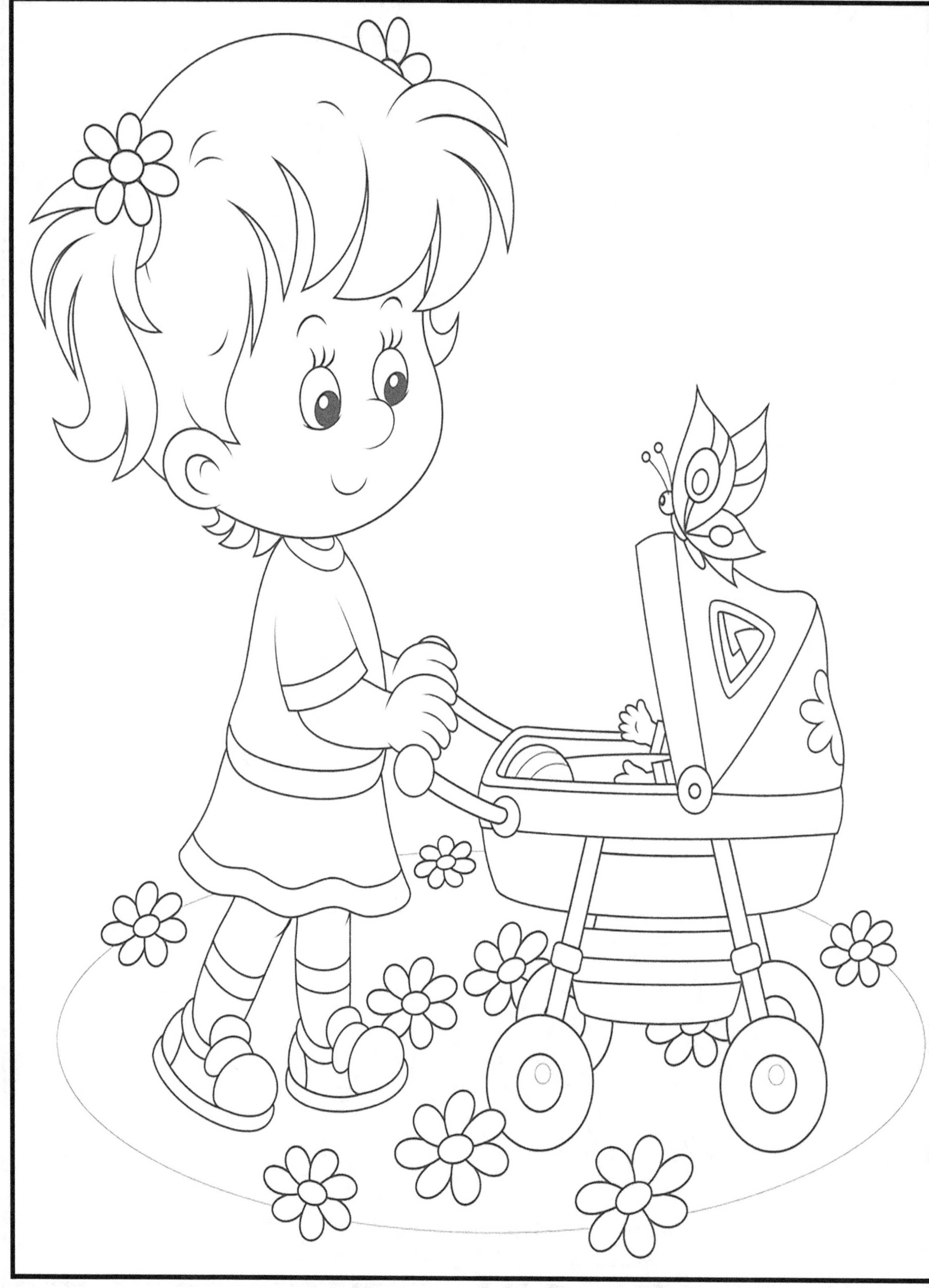

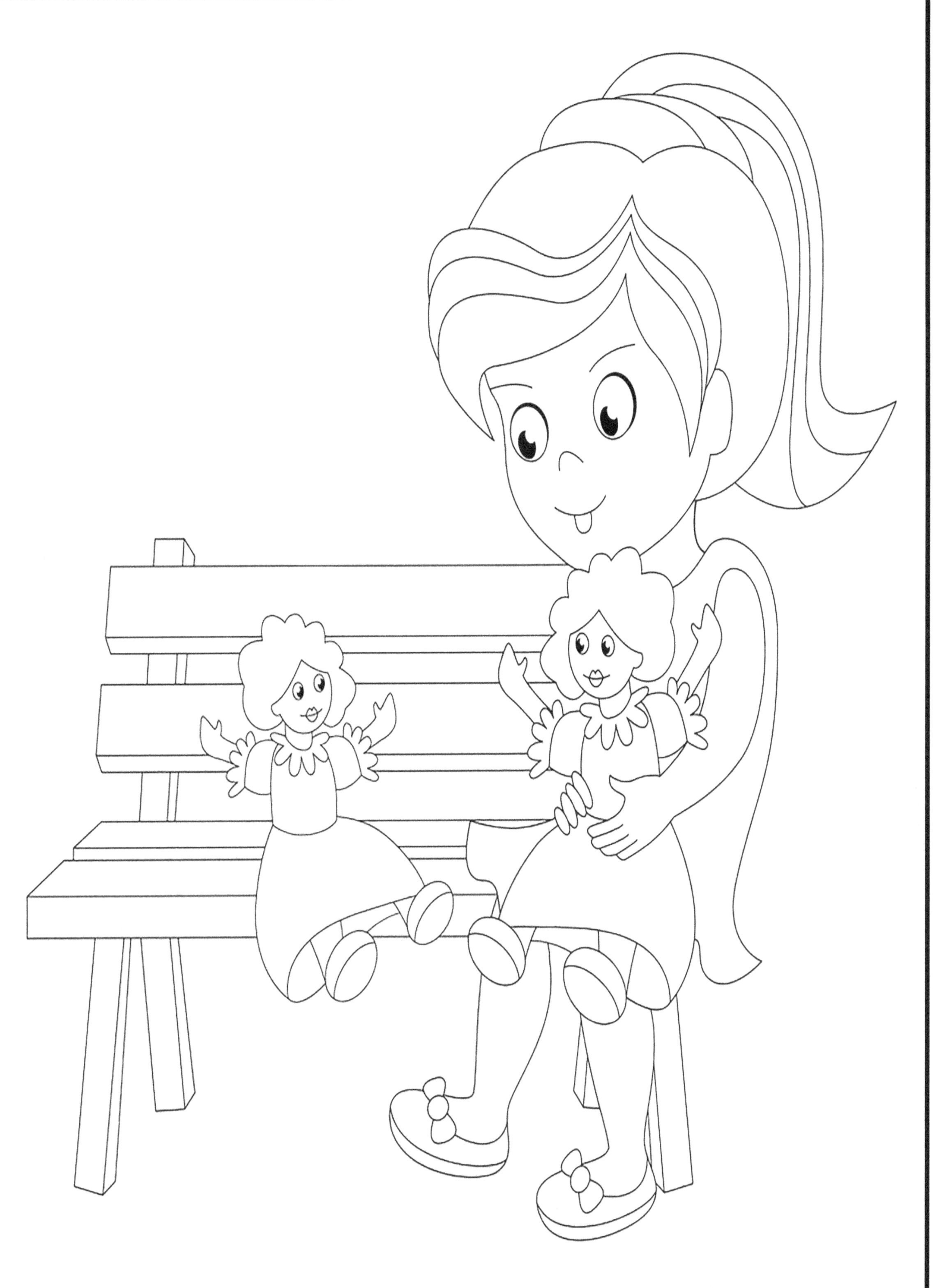

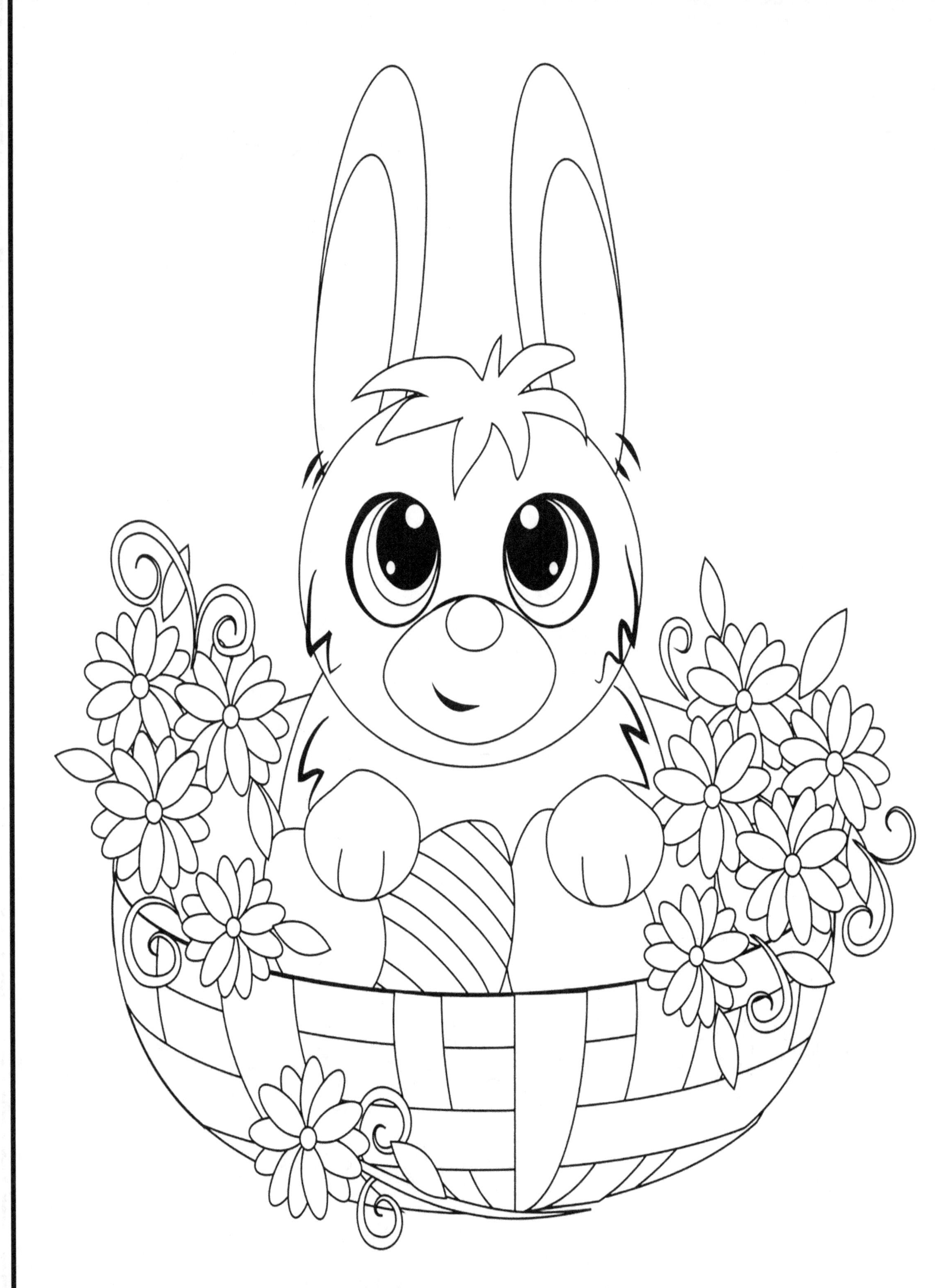

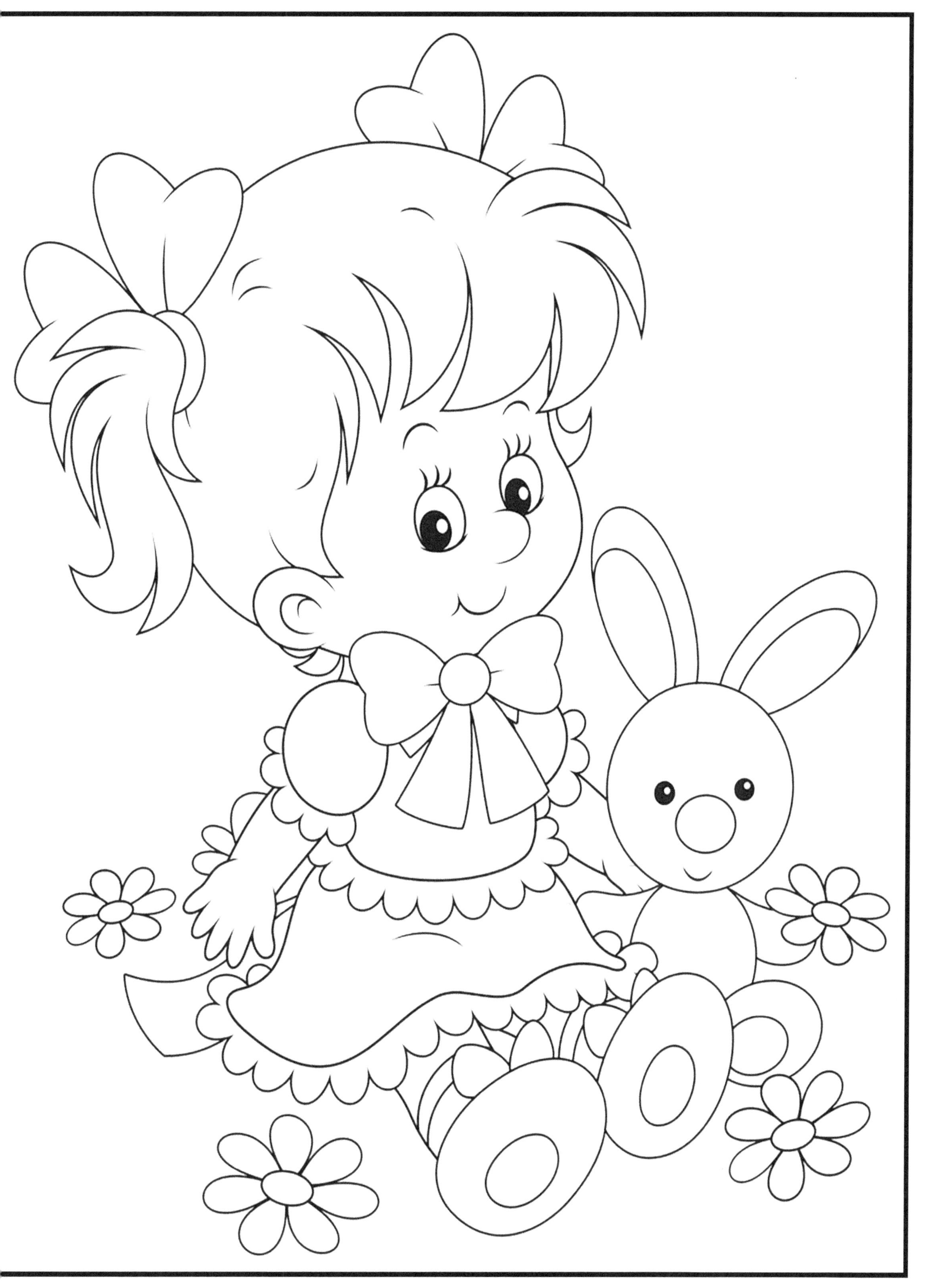

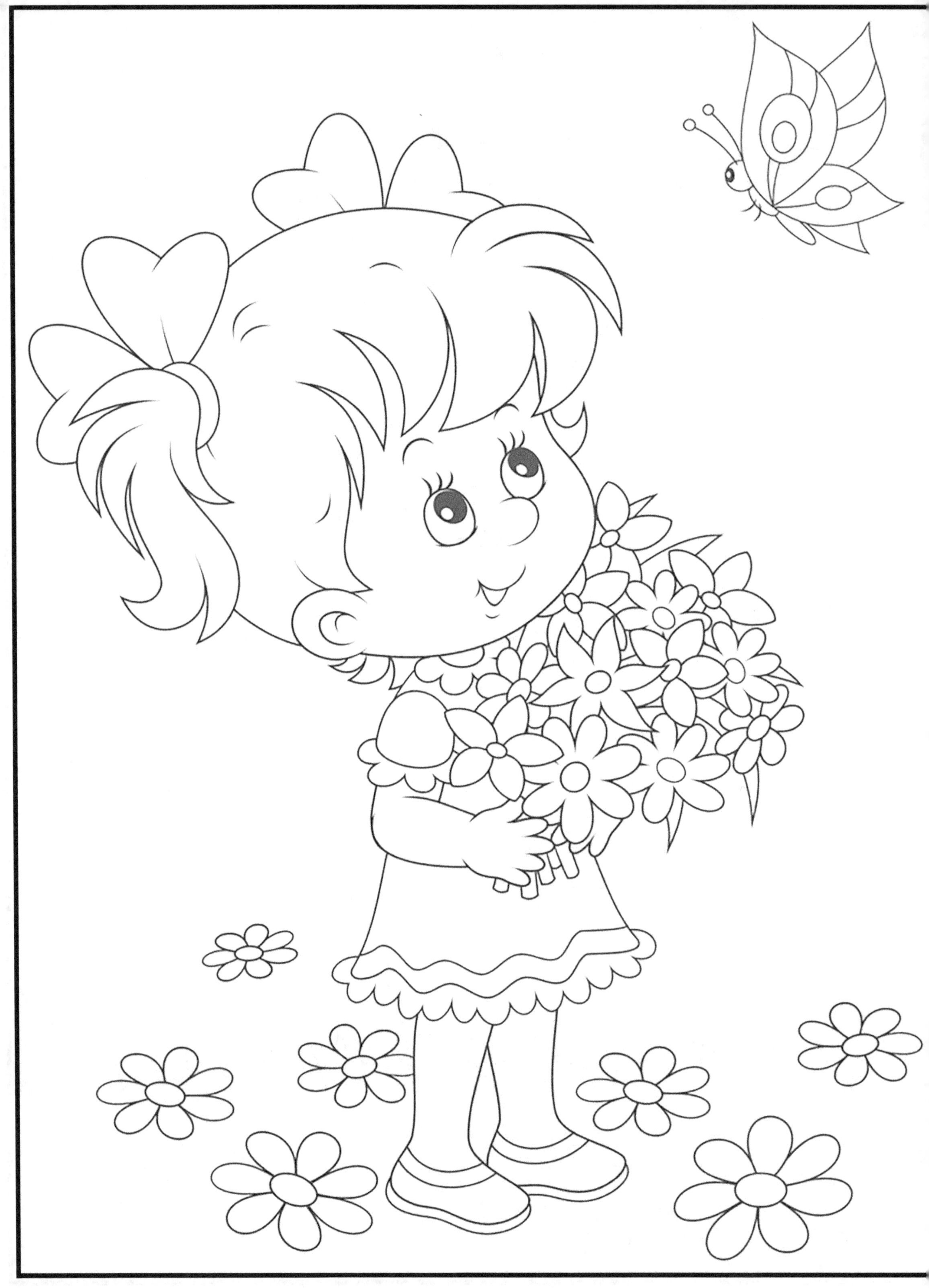

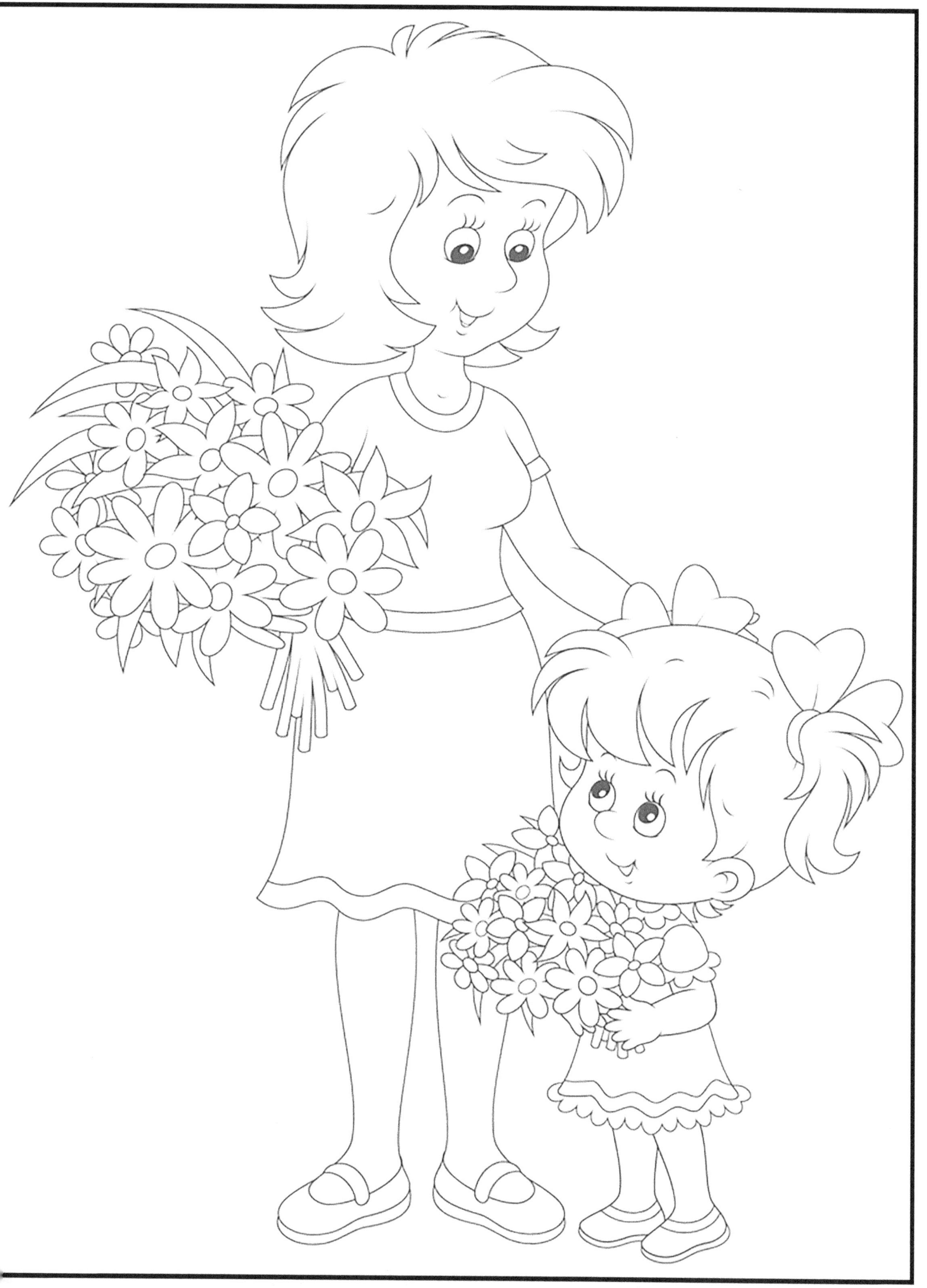

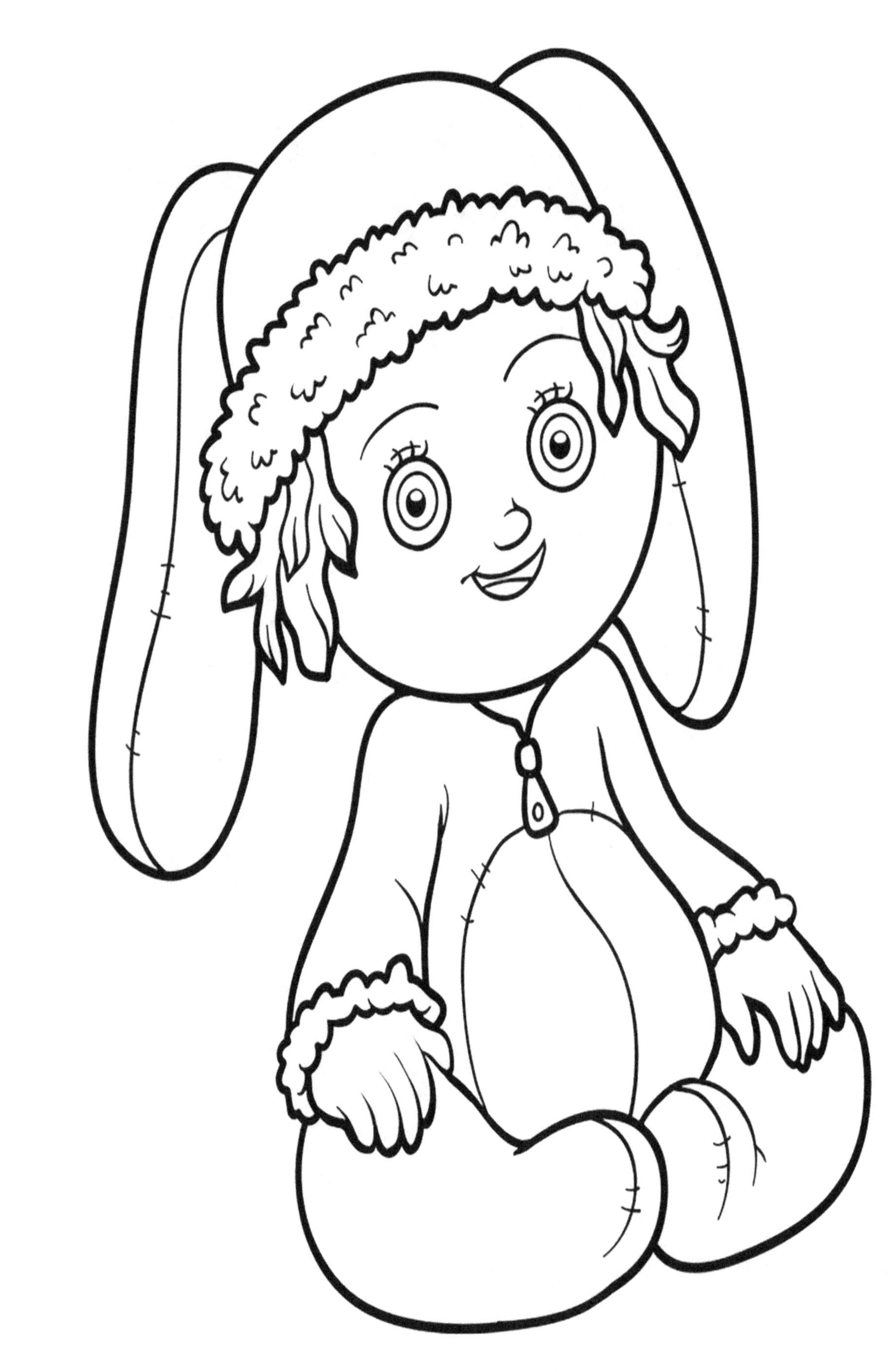

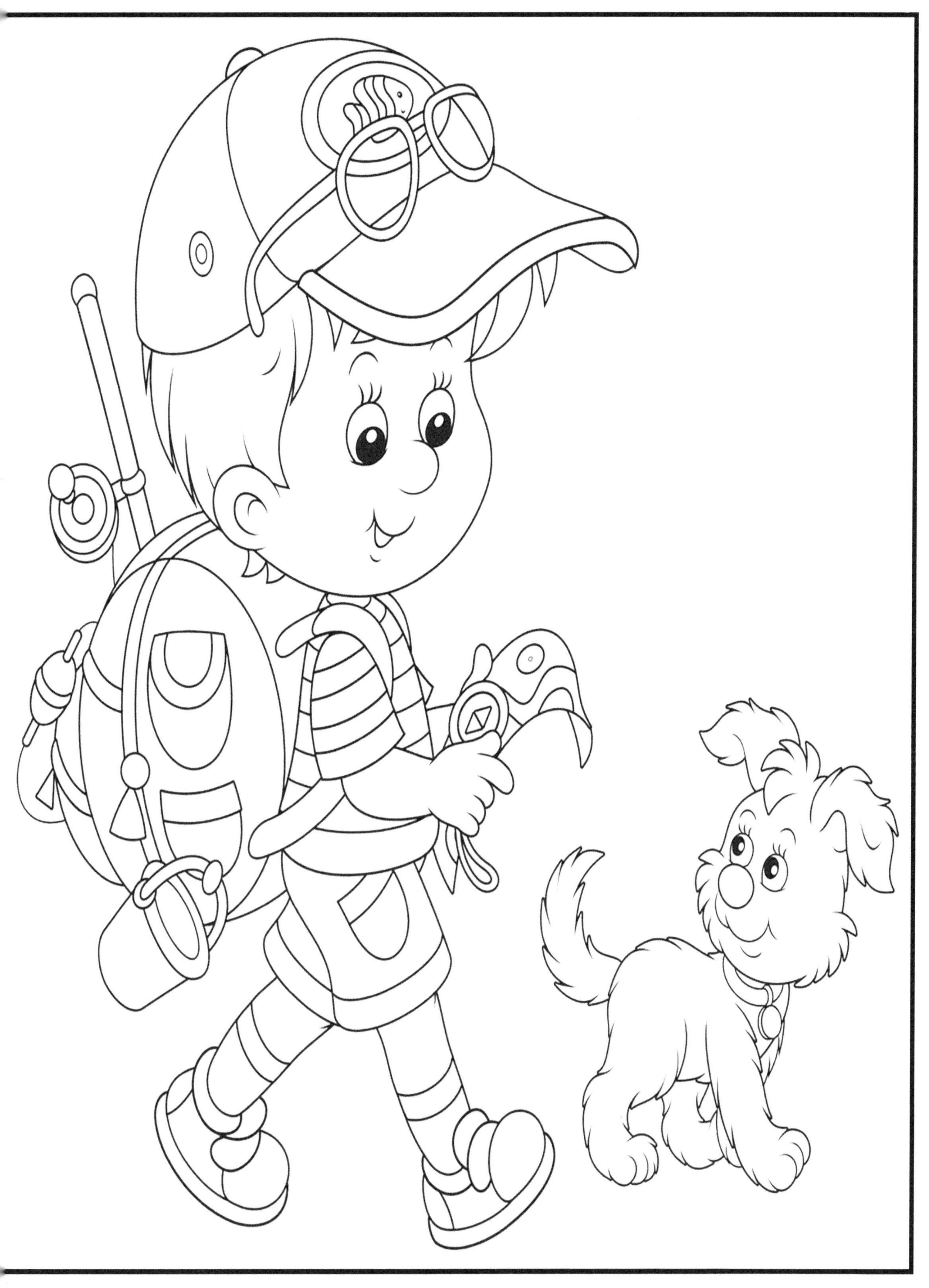

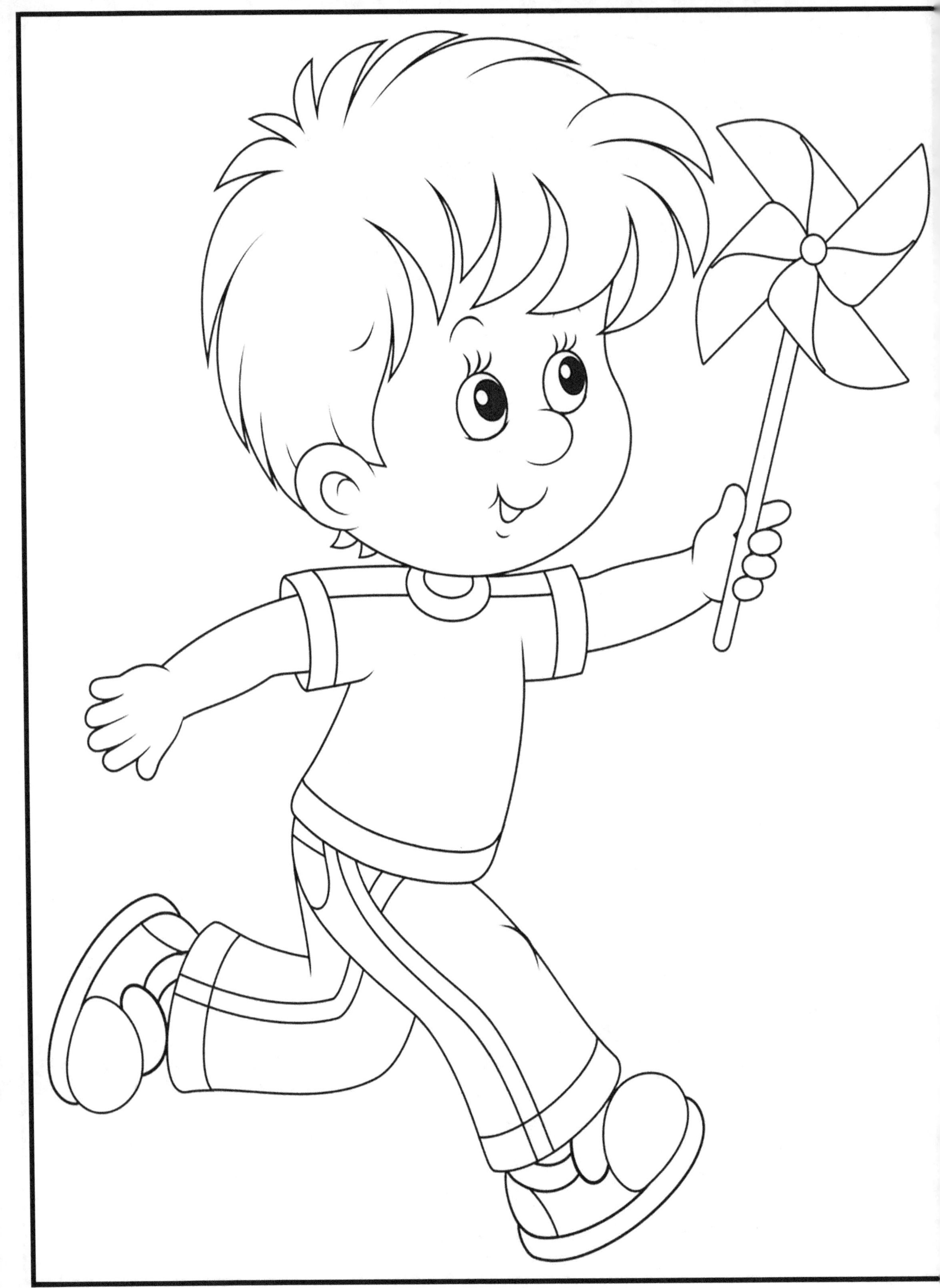

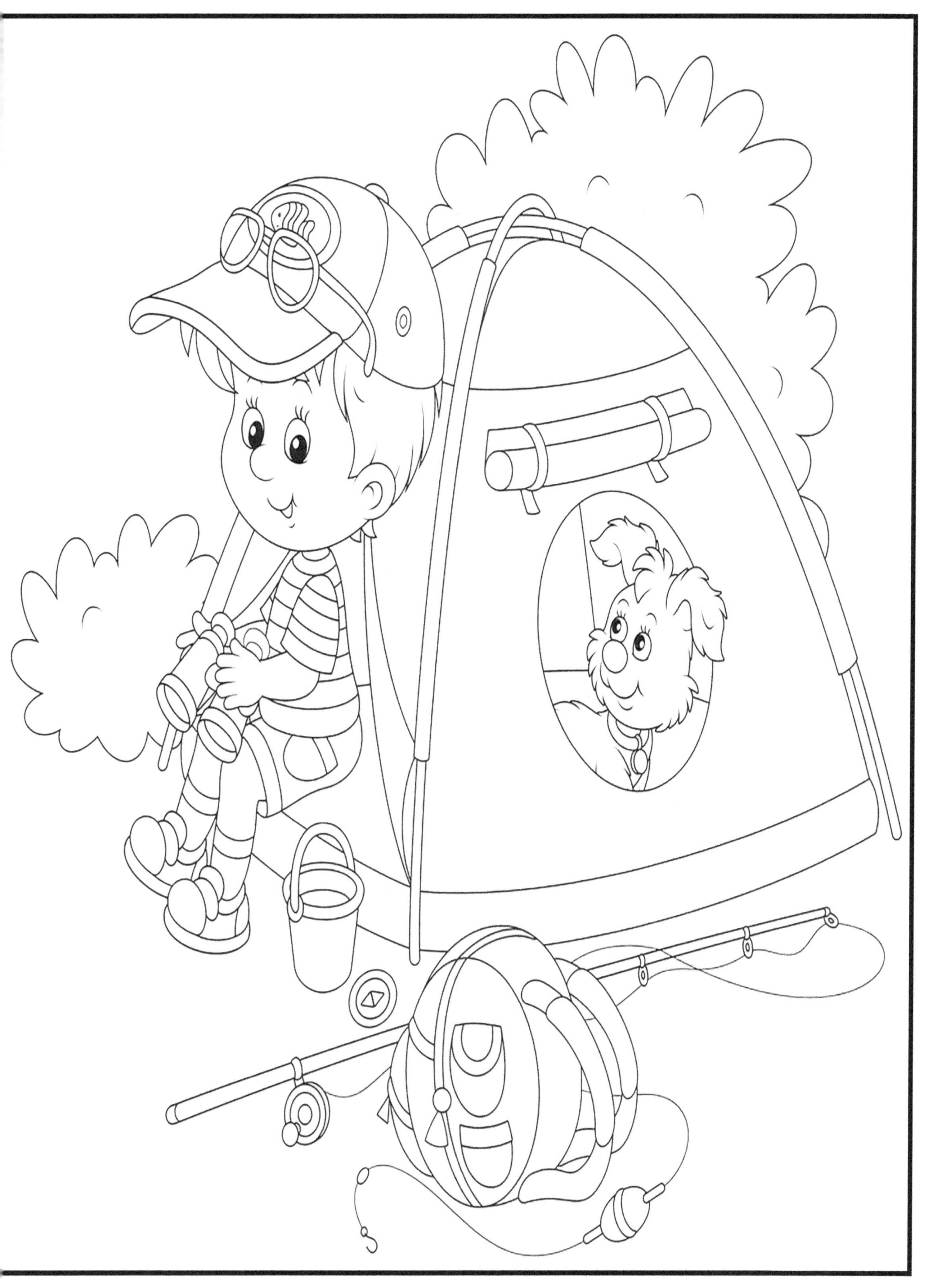

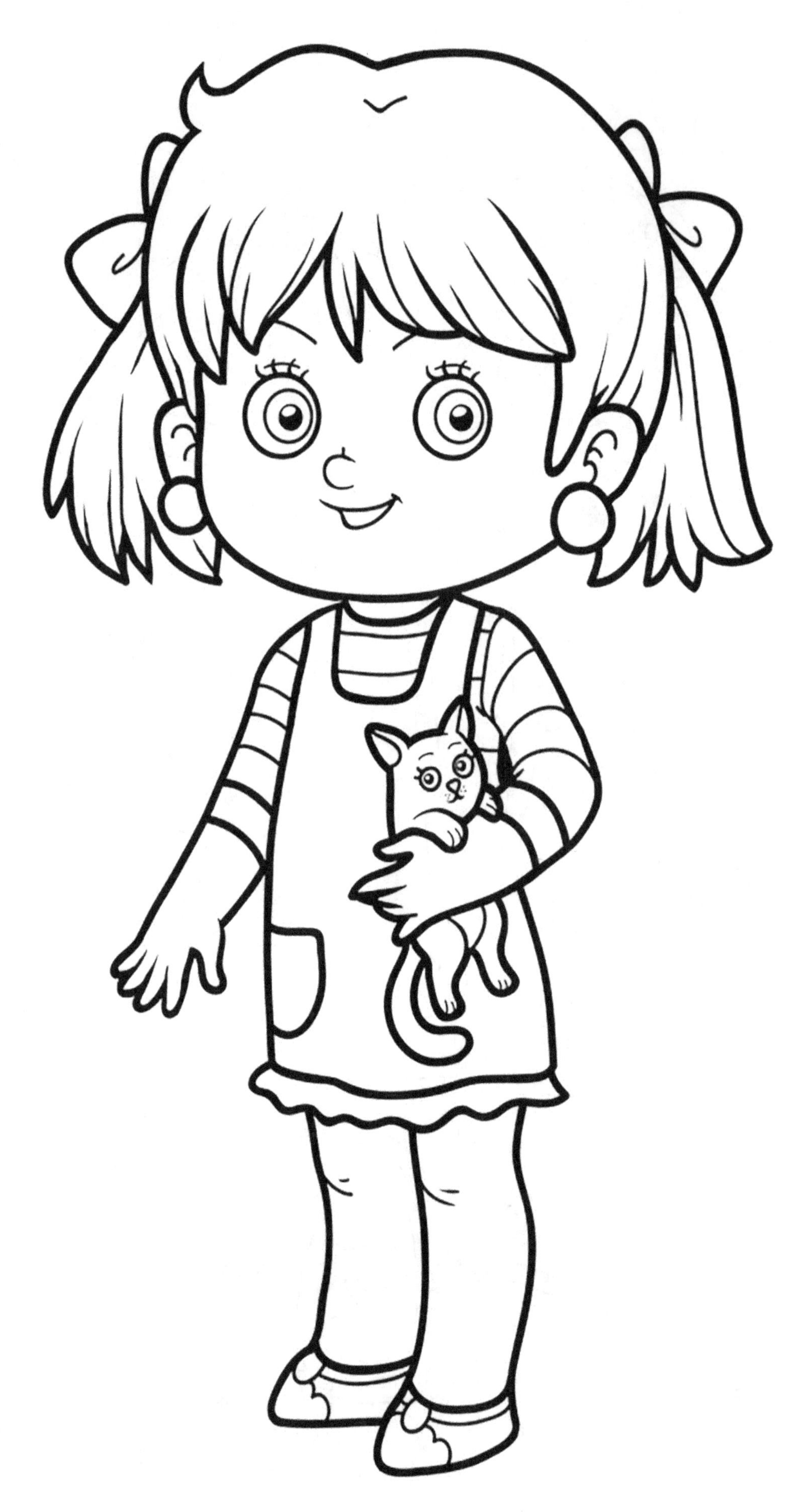

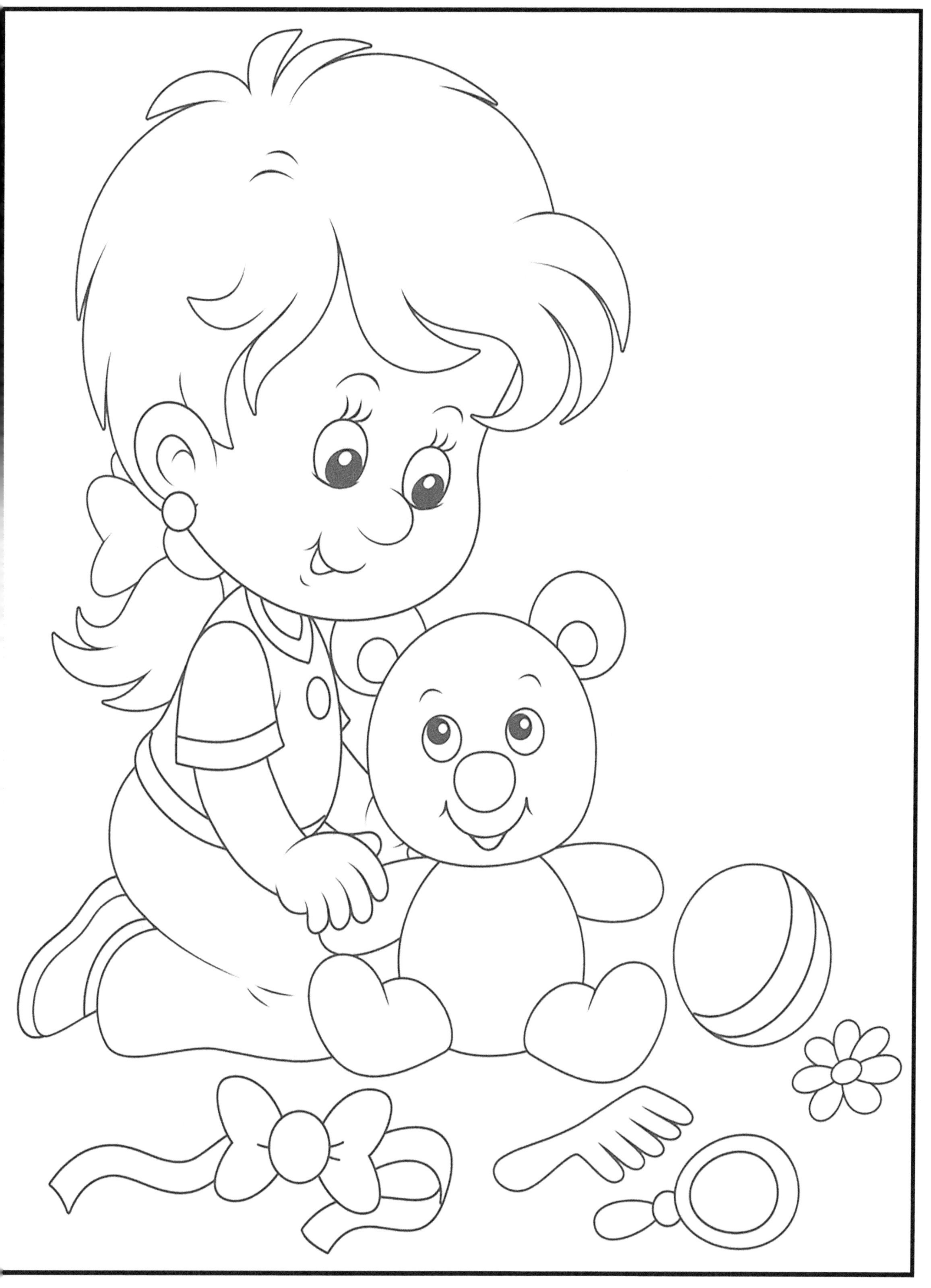

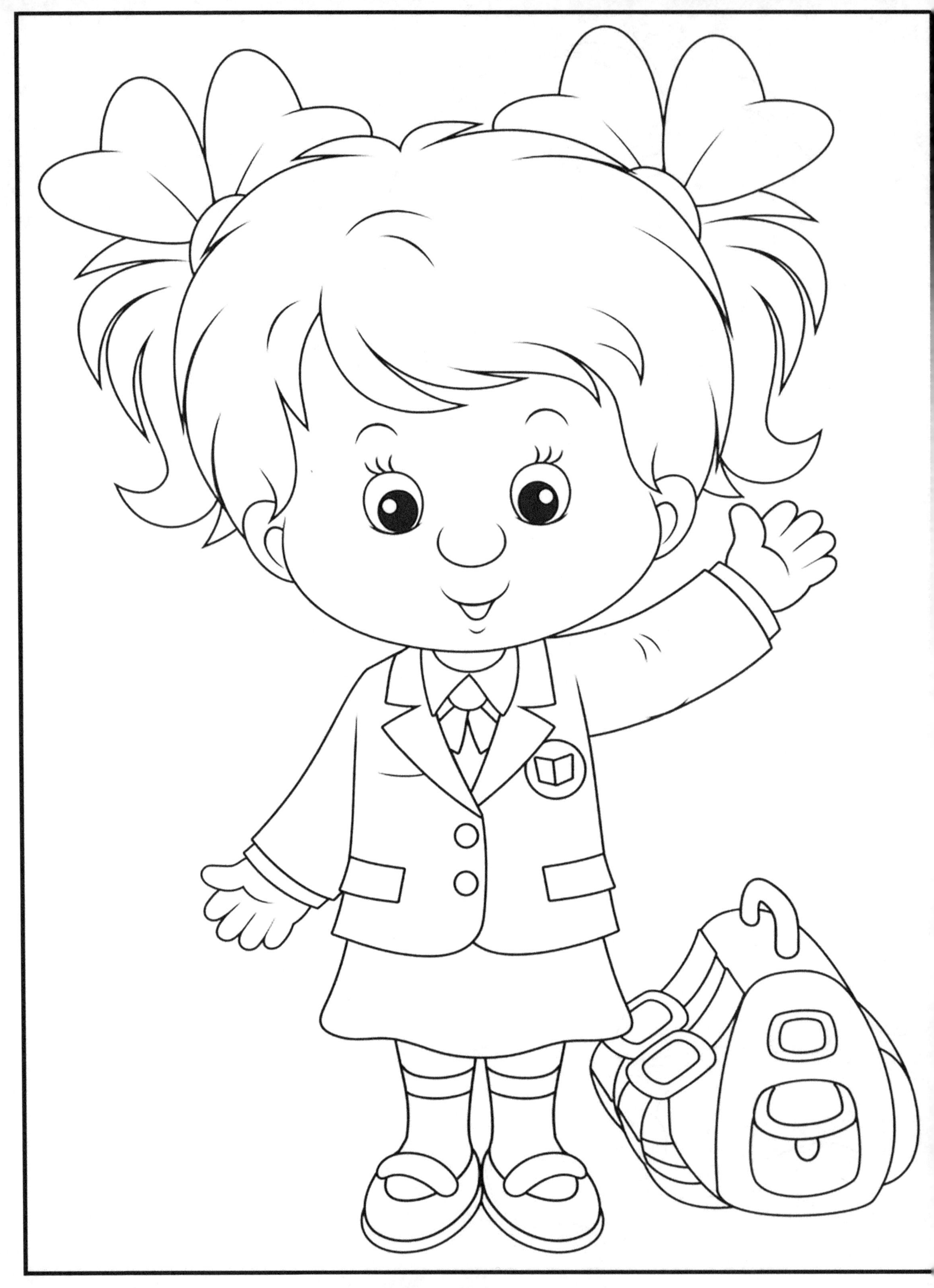

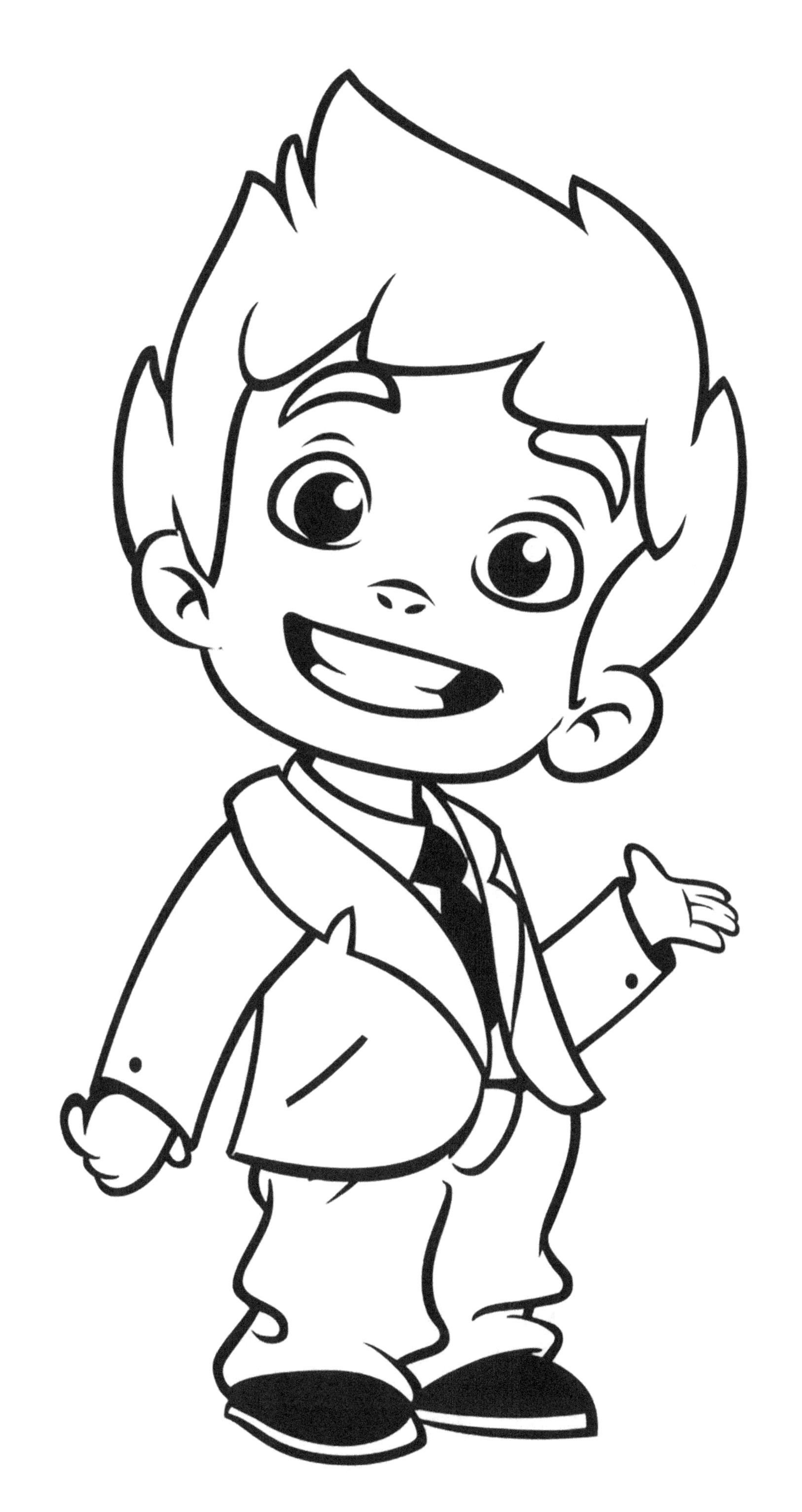

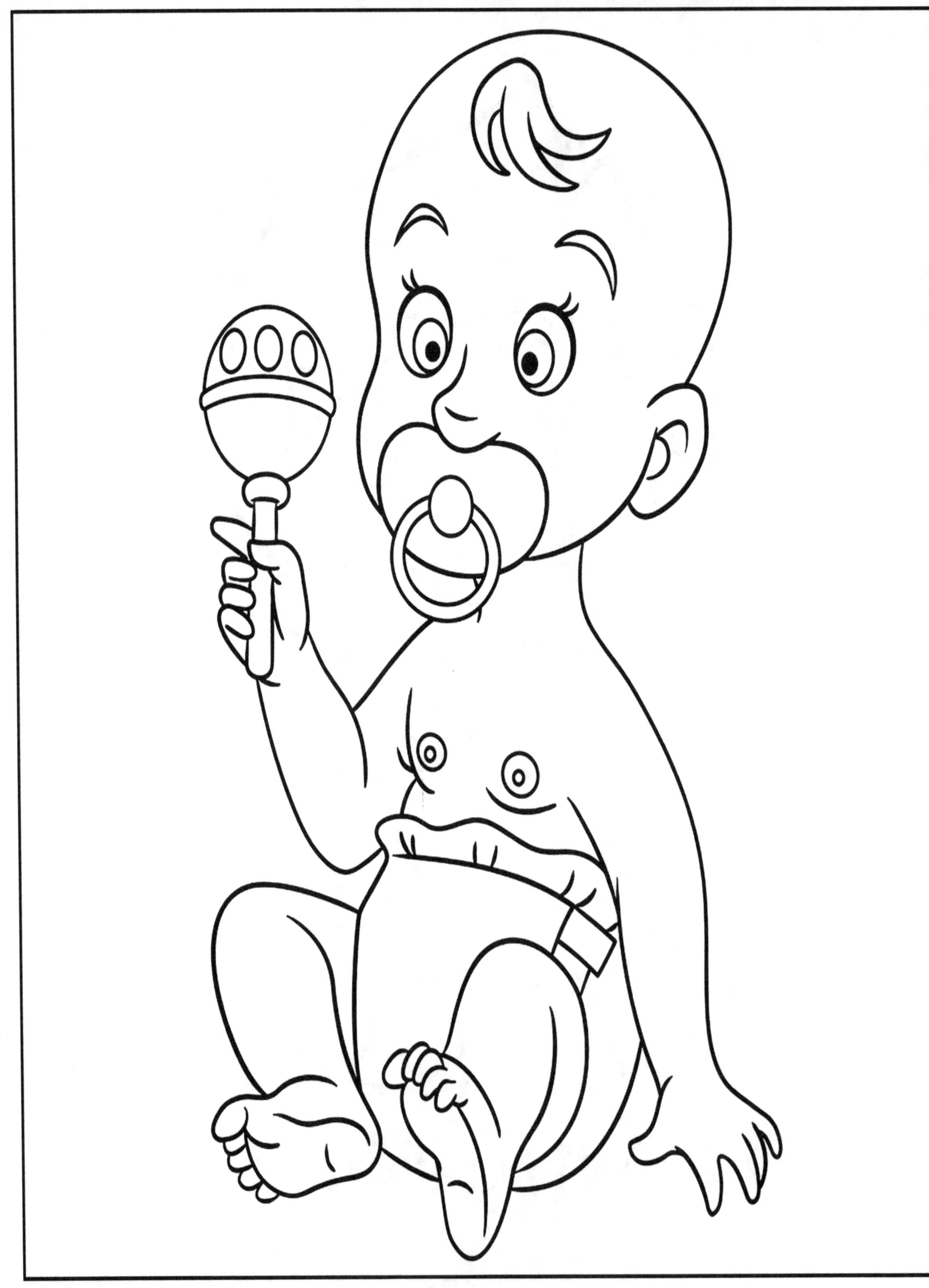

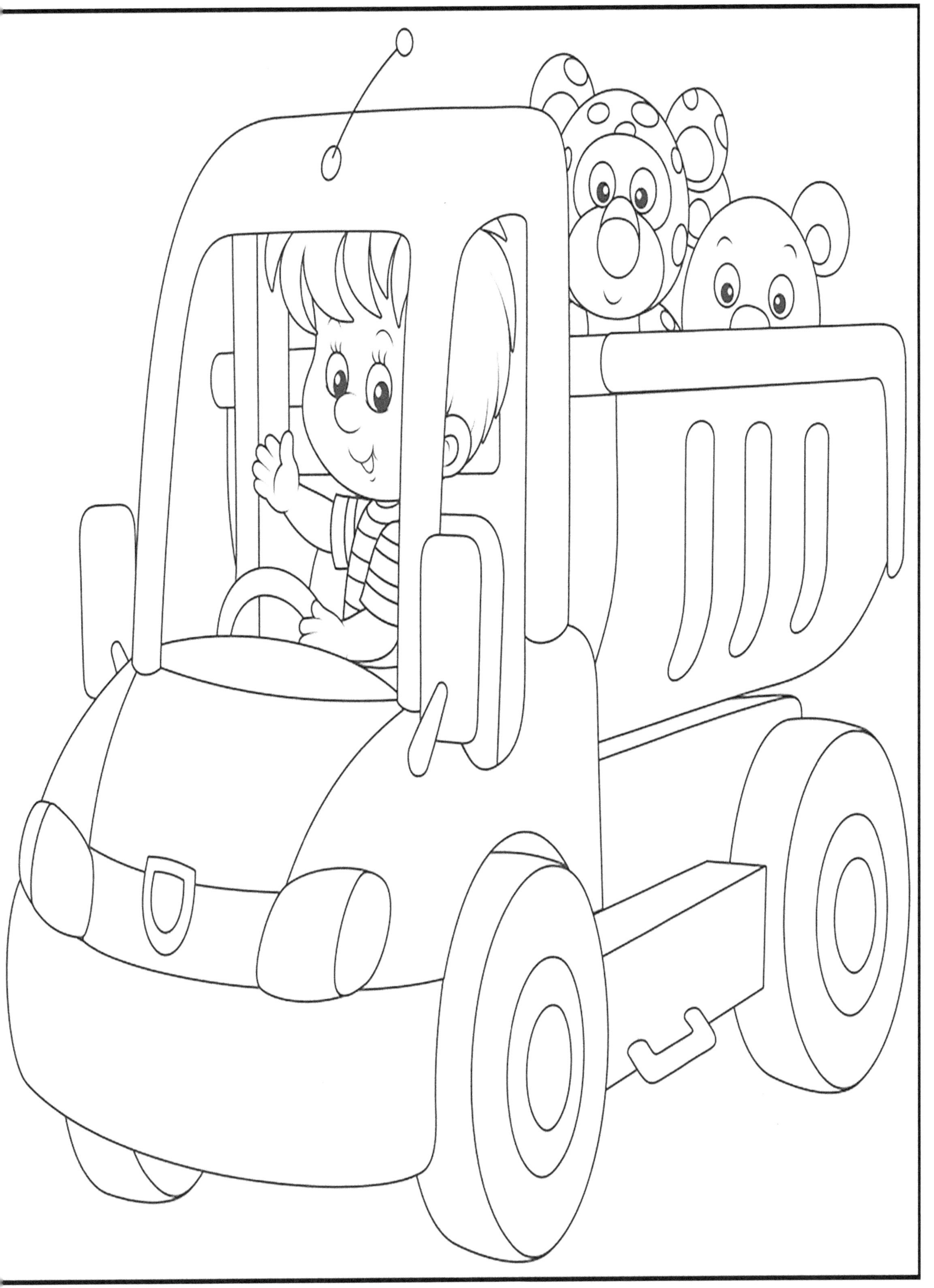

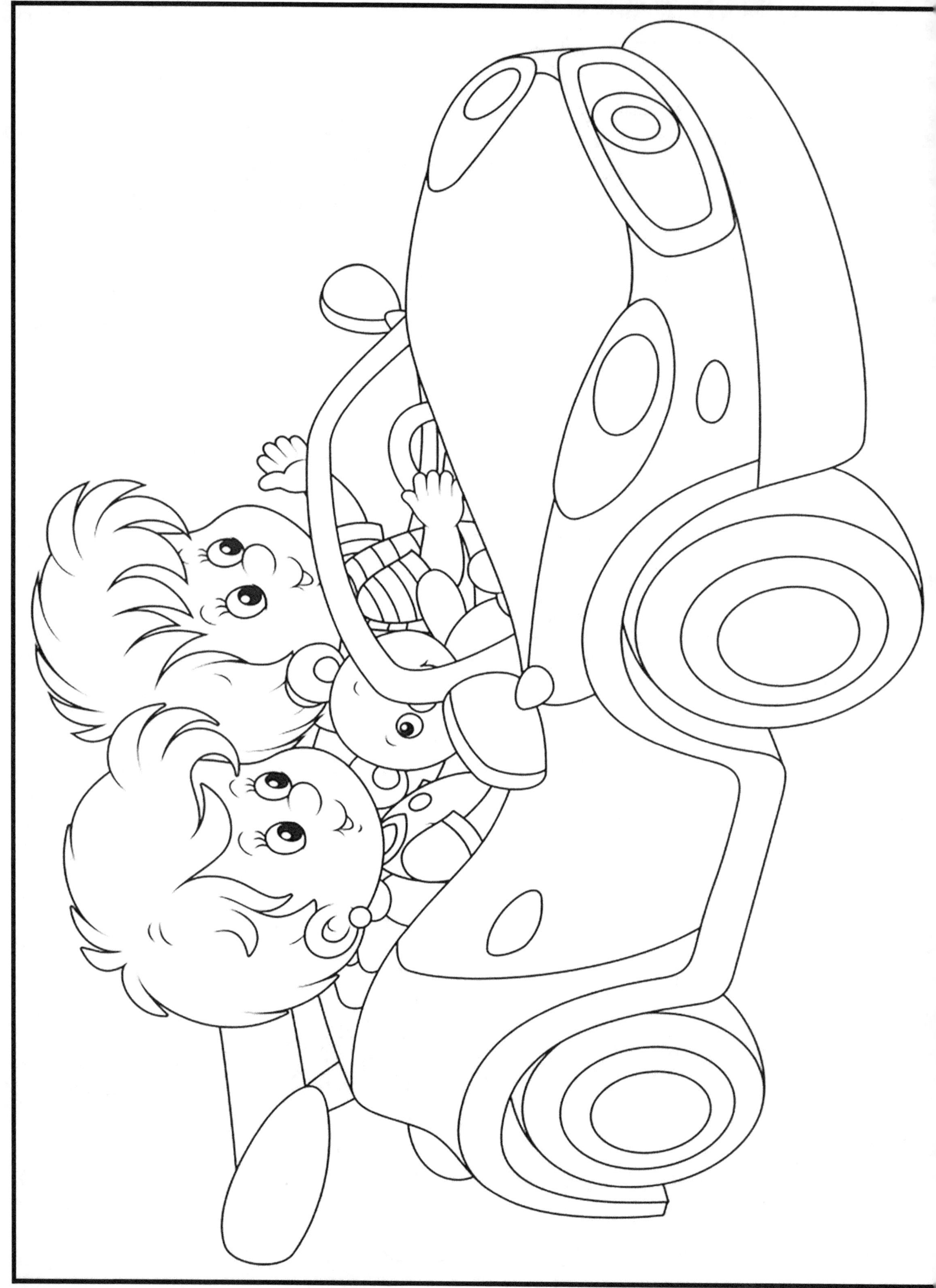

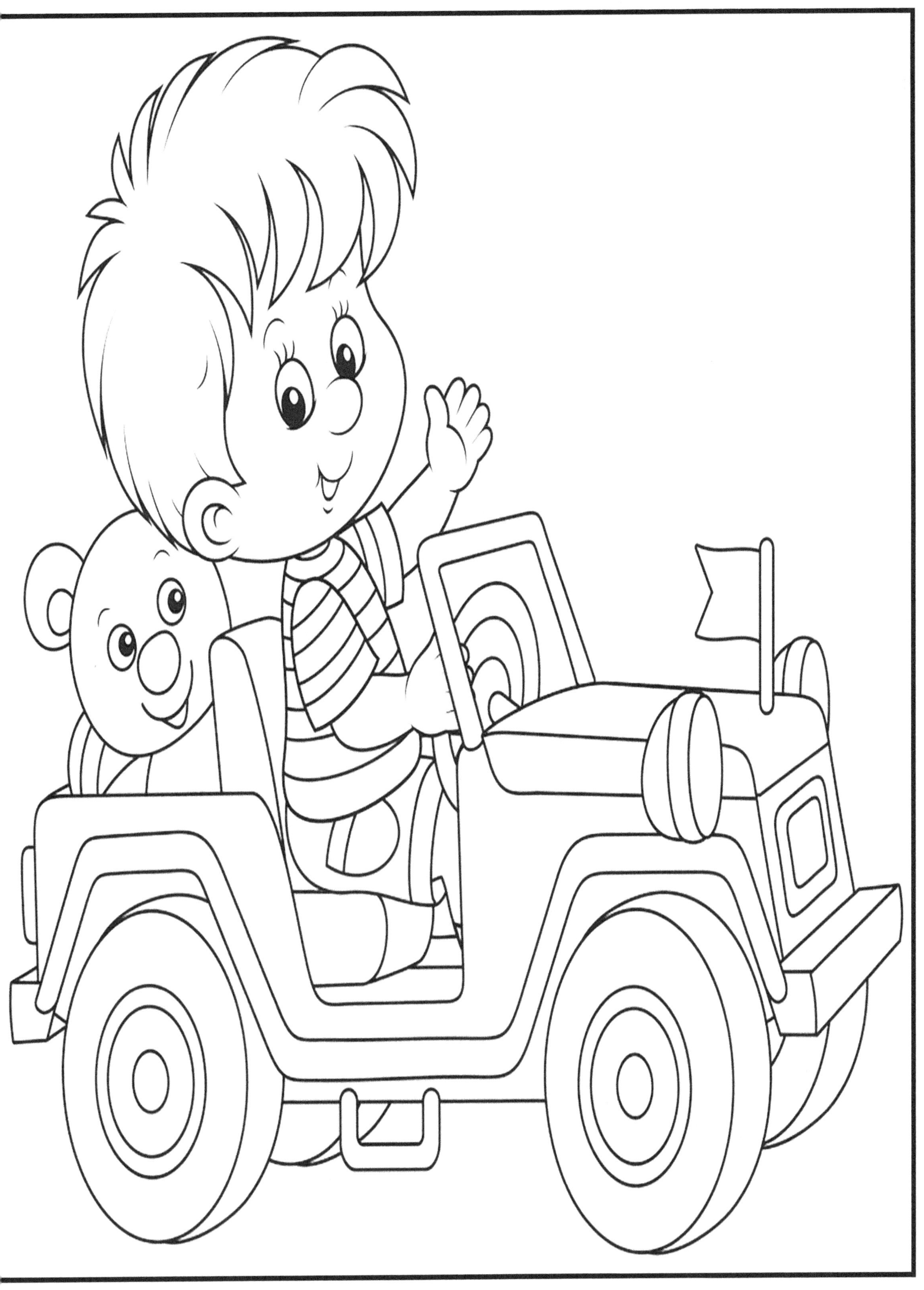

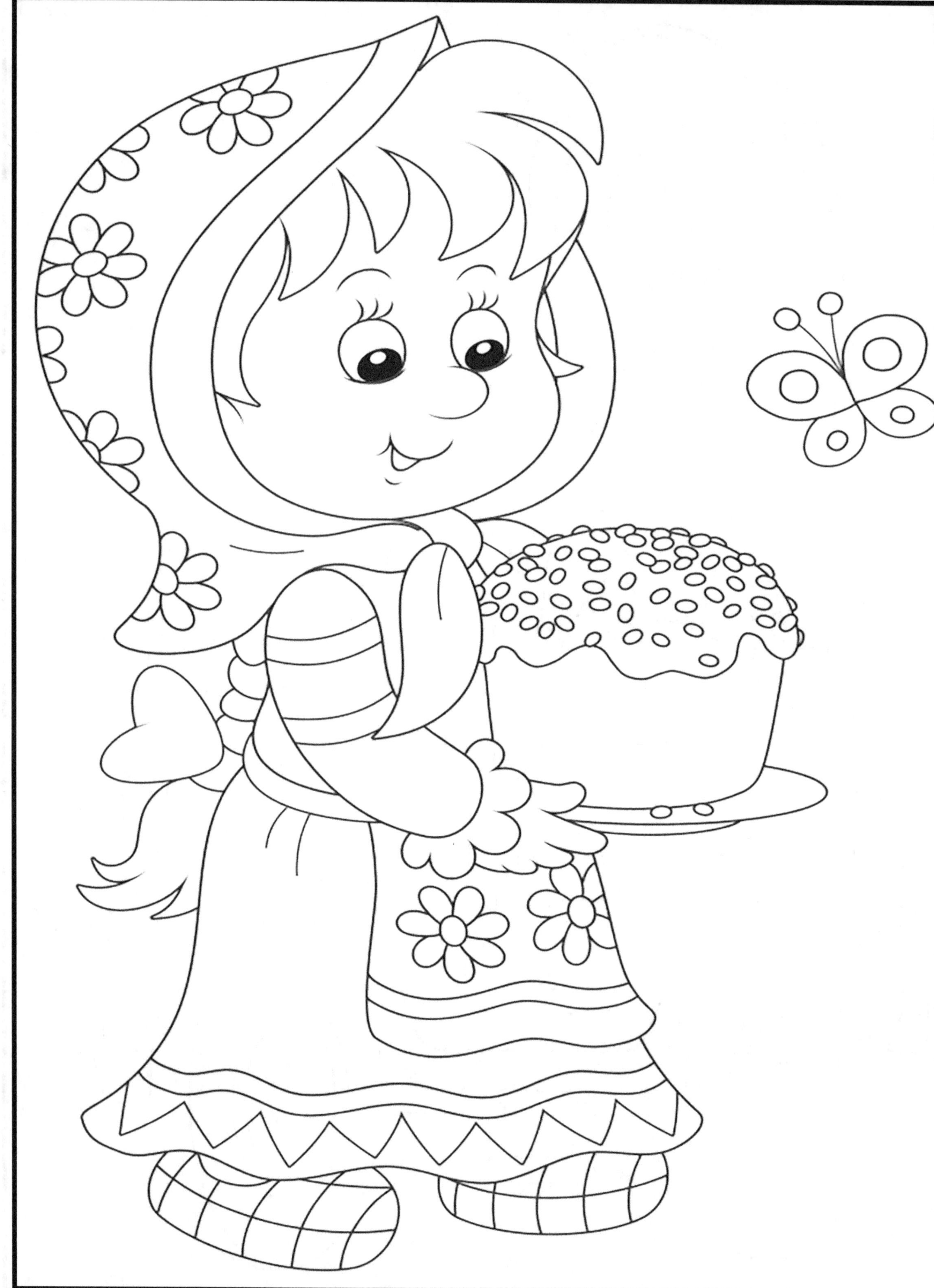